Dave —
Every Blessi
walk this road w
M Silva Gal. 6:9

#1 MAN

**WHAT EVERY DAD DESIRES.
WHAT EVERY DAUGHTER NEEDS.**

MIKE SILVA
FATHER OF FOUR DAUGHTERS

© 2011 Mike Silva International

Published by Mike Silva International
PO Box 8808, Portland, OR 97207

Printed in the United States of America

All rights reserved. No part of this publication may be reproduced, stored in a retrieval system, or transmitted in any form by any means, electronic, mechanical, photocopy, recording, or otherwise, without the prior permission of the publisher. The only exception is brief excerpts used for review purposes only.

Unless otherwise marked, all Scripture references are from the Holy Bible, New International Version®. Copyright © 1973, 1978, 1984 Biblica. Used by permission of Zondervan. All rights reserved.

Scripture references marked NASB are from the New American Standard Bible®. Copyright © 1960, 1962, 1963, 1968, 1971, 1972, 1973, 1975, 1977, 1995 by The Lockman Foundation. Used by permission.

Scripture quotations marked (AMP) are taken from the *Amplified Bible*, Copyright © 1954, 1958, 1962, 1964, 1965, 1987 by The Lockman Foundation. Used by permission.

ISBN 978-0-557-84533-0

www.mikesilva.org

Next to my Bride, Crystal . . . you're looking
at my four greatest accomplishments!

My girls: Loving you with all that I am is
now paying HUGE dividends that I may
not deserve, but am fully enjoying!

"BLESSED INDEED IS THE MAN WHO HEARS MANY GENTLE VOICES CALL HIM FATHER."

-LYDIA M. CHILD

ACKNOWLEDGMENTS

A special thank you to my friend Bradley Burck for helping make this book—a longtime dream of mine—a reality.

Many thanks to my girls, Jenna, Delight, Grace, and Kristianna for your significant insights and female perspectives. "Sam" and "Mary," thank you for allowing us to encourage and equip others because of your transparency.

To my Crystal, the rock of our family, the love of my life, and beautiful mother to our amazing daughters: I'll never fully be able to express the depth of my gratitude for you, but I'll spend the rest of my days trying.

Finally, to my friend and inspiration in so many ways, Max Lucado. Max, your endorsement on my life makes me feel like Lancelot when King Arthur knighted him! Thank you!

CONTENTS

Preface: Why Me?

1	It All Starts with You	1
2	Lavish with Acceptance	9
3	Off the Deep End: Wayward Children	21
4	Relationships and Your Girl	37
5	Biological vs. Stepfather Dynamic	53
6	Bad Labels and Communication	65
7	Myth Busters: Fact & Fiction About Dads and Daughters	77
8	16 Life Saving Steps	89
9	Why We Need Each Other	105
	Epilogue: No Greater Love	113

"A TRULY RICH MAN IS ONE WHOSE CHILDREN RUN INTO HIS ARMS WHEN HIS HANDS ARE EMPTY."

- UNKNOWN

PREFACE: WHY ME?

I'm so angry at her I can't even speak right now. In fact, if she were not my daughter, she would never be my friend! Have you ever felt this desperate for help and encouragement on this roller-coaster ride of parenting daughters? The only thing that gives me credibility to write a book like this is that I have made so many mistakes parenting; it's taken me this long to compile my list! Unconditional love, plus time, plus life experience, divided by a wise wife times God's grace equals…the most wonderful fulfilling relationship with all four of my (now adult) daughters who not only call me Daddy, but friend! As you read these thoughts and reflections about my adventures of parenting daughters, I pray you may relate and, most of all, not feel alone. Dads, we are on this journey together. Please allow the Lord God to inspire you and me to assist you as we navigate the sometimes mysterious, always surprising world of daughters!

All of us would like to be our girl's (or girls') hero, right? Through the years, I've moved up and down the spectrum of importance in their lives and thus I've learned a thing or two. Things that I have recorded here will hopefully be for your benefit.

The worst thing we can do is give up on our daughter or ourselves. So may today be the day that we say "no" to the negativity that paralyzes us. Together, let's be the one thing she needs most in life…her daddy to be her #1 man.

"HE DIDN'T TELL ME HOW TO LIVE;
HE LIVED, AND LET ME
WATCH HIM DO IT."

- CLARENCE BUDINGTON KELLARD

1

IT ALL STARTS WITH YOU

Most of us mimic what we see. We learn by watching. From infancy, our family, friends, and culture shape and conform us into who we are as people. As men, husbands, and especially fathers, we often don't realize that we too are being watched, mimicked, and followed. If your daughter could turn on the television and watch how you live when you *think* nobody is watching would you be ashamed? I would at times. (Have you seen Jim Carey's *The Truman Show*? That's what the movie is about.)

Fathers, thirst for integrity. Pursue the high road in private. Seek God's heart for wisdom to lead. Get a bulldog grip on a commitment to unconditional love. Bottom line, live as if people are watching you...because she is!

As someone who lived in Hawaii working and going to school, it's no surprise that I love the beach, warm ocean water, and lots of sunshine. Unfortunately, I now understand a clear lesson about parenting that I learned from all that sun. Crystal and I have confirmed: what we (parents) do in moderation our children will generally do in excess! Did you catch that? Please read it again.

Here's how that principle applies to me in this example. I did not use sunscreen in my Hawaiian days; however, I wanted my daughters to use it. As you can imagine, telling the girls to use SPF 60 sunscreen when I was unwilling to wear it myself rendered me ineffective in that area. I wanted them to do what I said, not what I did.

Fathers, if this describes you, I have two words for you: Good luck! My friend, James Ryle, hit the nail on the head when he said, "Your children may not always heed your advice, but they will never escape your influence." With that in mind, here are a few ideas to encourage you. Try giving:

A little more love: When my girls were in certain stages, it's funny how I so easily saw their weaknesses. I noticed impatience, selfishness, pride, cheating, and other shortcomings. One day, the light came on for me. I realized that every fault I noticed in my daughters had been alive in me at one time or another. The only difference was my "eyesight." My acute vision with their weaknesses ignored blindness to my own flaws. If you can relate, ask your daughter for forgiveness. Then exchange judgment and ridicule for a little more love.

A little more joy: Work stress, finances, extended family issues, marriage, car troubles, *plus* fathering three teenage girls at the same time is a lot to carry.

The difference between happiness and joy is that happiness is based on our present circumstances. Joy, on the other hand, is not measured by circumstances. Joy is a choice. If your daughter is "killing you" right now and you feel attacked and deflated by her rather than loved and honored, choose joy. Why? Because what you now see in your daughter is *not* the final product! Like her father, she is a work in progress. Don't see her as she is today; see her as what she will become. I actually shared this with one of my girls, and it helped her attitude and the way she saw herself.

One of my friends has been described as someone who "spills joy" onto everyone he encounters. Do you think this man has heard only the answer "yes" and never "no"? Do you think doors have only opened for him and never closed? I know that's not the case. So what's the key to having a response like his? It's a choice. Choose joy, and eventually you'll have enough of it to spill over onto others too—guaranteed!

A little more peace: Two of our girls were fighting and arguing back and forth. It seemed like it would never stop. I felt exhausted. The only thing I wanted to do was run away but decided not to because I knew when I came back home they would still be fighting!

With maturity comes a little more peace. Our peace cannot depend upon the ups and downs of a teenage girl. Be the parent. Allow her to be the daughter. Be consistent. Why? Because with consistency, you will be what she needs but simply doesn't realize yet. Gentlemen, like you, throughout the years I have had some difficult seasons with my girls. I've gone on record as saying the more I got to know my teenager, the more I loved my dog. Need some peace at your home? Take a walk outside—it simply may be around the block.

A little more patience: I remember the first time I had to change a diaper. To keep from losing my cool, I put Jimmy Piersall's baseball diaper-changing method into action: "Spread the diaper in the position of a baseball diamond with you at bat. Then fold second base down to home and set the baby on the pitcher's mound. Put first base and third together, bring up home plate, and pin the three together. Of course, in case of rain, you get to call the game and start all over again." Seriously, we can find the energy and staying power to parent teenage girls today because, like the babies we once diapered, they will not stay that way forever. Patience, my friend, is a graduate virtue. Model patience so your daughter will extend it to her own children some day.

A little more kindness/goodness/gentleness: When our youngest came, I had work and Crystal had three other girls to care for, plus we were in the middle of a major move. Kindness, goodness, and gentleness were all qualities I needed but lacked. Funny how we're put in situations that bring forth character traits we need. Though uncomfortable, we become better people through those times. Muscle only grows through resistance.

A little more self-control: At times one of the girls would insist on doing things her way. If I had it to do over again, I would have prayed for more balance and discretion, because life experience has taught me that acting like a marine corps drill sergeant is highly ineffective with young girls. Thank God that "love covers a multitude of sins" (1 Pet. 4:8). Gentlemen, it's because of my experience that I'm able to share these things with you. I feel as though I've made ample mistakes in parenting our daughters. Please learn from my blunders. One thing I know for sure—my ace card is that I love my girls. Make a mistake, lose my cool, and overreact? When I follow up with an apology and a loving embrace, lo and behold, fellowship is restored.

How does this happen? Because love covers over my wrongs. Love promotes healing in little girls' hearts. Love diminishes my errors. Do you see it? My relationship with my daughters is a picture of my relationship with my heavenly Father. I make mistakes, wrong turns, negative choices, and yet because God's Son, Jesus Christ, died on the cross, His shed blood eliminates all of my wrongdoing and sin. The question, men, is: Why? Why would my heavenly Father do this for me, for us? The answer: Love. In like fashion, the way His love covers my errors, our love for our daughters covers our less-than-perfect actions and attitudes.

Imagine what life would be like if we each had just a little bit more self-control. It's good to step back and think about the small ways we can grow spiritual fruit in our lives: the fruit of love, joy, peace, patience, and *self-*

control. Our daughters' best shot at self-control is when they see it in our lives. That thought motivates me to the max! Parenting is tough work. I wish it were as easy as one-two-three and a snap of my fingers. Unfortunately, it's not.

My daughters have watched and observed me for so long that many of my worst habits could become second nature to them. That's why we must lead by example. If you don't want your kids to do something wrong or negative, don't do it yourself.

In the movie *The Truman Show*, a character tells Truman, "Everything that's happening to you is real. What you don't know is that someone's watching you." What a powerful wake-up call for us.

Dads, if you want your daughter to love you, then love her sacrificially and unconditionally. If you want her to be a kind, faithful servant, show her how. Too many of us don't walk the talk. Today, however, is your opportunity to start over.

ACTION STEPS

☑ Live like you're being watched 24/7, because, in reality, you are.

☑ Incorporate spiritual fruit into every area of your life—you'll be amazed at the difference this makes.

☑ Walk the talk! Hypocritical lifestyles are a dead-end street.

"THE REAL QUESTION IS NOT WHETHER OR NOT YOU LOVE YOUR KIDS, BUT HOW WELL YOU ARE ABLE TO DEMONSTRATE YOUR LOVE SO THAT YOUR CHILDREN REALLY FEEL LOVED."

- STEPHANIE MARSTON

2

LAVISH WITH ACCEPTANCE

I'm learning that no matter how many girls are in your family, each is unique. Different styles, dress, humor…each is original. But be sure of this: every daughter shares the desire to be accepted by the people in her life. And if acceptance doesn't fall in her lap, she will do whatever it takes to seek it out. I learned this by watching our daughters grow up.

Jenna, my oldest, was the outgoing, fun, people person who everyone loved. She was driven, independent, creative, spontaneous, and, according to her mother, was just like me. Hey, that's not all bad, is it?

In her younger years, Delight was quiet, shy, and practically mute.

Extremely shy doesn't even begin to describe her. Then high school hit—and bam! We had a firecracker on our hands. If you wanted to know what Delight was thinking, just ask her and she would tell you. In fact, there was no need to ask her opinion. She would tell you anyway!

Grace was our sweet, affectionate, emotional, creative girl who loved loving and loved to be loved. She appeared sweet and innocent (on the outside), but press the right button and she could be downright feisty.

Kristianna was personality-plus—entertainer, comedian, master of persuasion, and CFO of Daddy's wallet!

Individuality is what makes families fun, unique, and special. Yes, there are other unmentionable and unfavorable traits in each of us, but we are learning to take the good with the bad. What qualifies our family to even write a book like this is that we often messed up (our list of mistakes seems endless). But that's why I'm so thankful for Peter's words about love covering a multitude of sins.

My daughters would say, "When I'm a parent, I'm never going to do that!" And I'd tell them, "Be careful, Sweetheart. Ask yourself, 'Are you the kind of daughter that you're going to want to mother someday?' Why? Because you *will* get your chance!"

Forgive and Forget: The Key to Acceptance

Forgiveness is the only way to find release from the bondage of hurt, pain, anger, and resentment. Other things can cover it up for a while, but not permanently. It doesn't matter who you are, where you come from, or what language you speak, forgiveness is at the core of who we are as people. We all make mistakes; we must be able to go back to people who we love and who we've hurt and say, "I'm so sorry. Please forgive me."

A friend reminds me frequently, "We are all dysfunctional." Isn't that the truth? Parenting is going to get better when we realize that we don't have it all together (our daughters don't either), and it's time we make a pact with our girls to do this thing called *life* together, arm in arm. Tell your daughters, "I'll watch your back and you watch mine. I will love you unconditionally and accept you for who you are (note: that's a two-way street, ladies) and we'll make it through this thing together."

We must not hold on to past mistakes. If we have apologized and forgiven each other, let it go! Life is too short to hold on to grudges. "But what she did is unforgivable!" you may say. "I'll never be able to forget and move on." It's easy to feel that way. Many of us have felt that way at some point in our lives, and we'll most likely feel it again. But what's done is done. Move on with our daughters and be restored in relationship with one another. Life experience has proven that to me. There is no relationship that is too far gone. Any amount of brokenness can be mended and restored. Two forgivers = one satisfied heart!

Take on the attitude of an Olympic athlete: Don't look back. Don't quit. Don't give up. Don't give in. For as long as it takes, fight the good fight until you reach the finish line, accomplish the goal, and attain the gold medal.

Imagine if we all lived this way. Choose the high road that leads to victory over the easy way out that leads to heartbreak and regret.

We want to protect our girls in every way. Whether it's mental, social, emotional, spiritual, or physical wellbeing, we want to keep her safe. We are jealous for our daughter's love and attention, and gladly pour our life into her. When she's old enough to drive and runs the car along the mailbox and the insurance deductible is $1,000, we get to pay it. Or, there is my personal favorite: when some guy waltzes into the picture and suddenly all my daughters were dreaming about *The Notebook*. They envisioned dancing in the street, receiving daily love letters, and taking boat rides on a pond surrounded by white swans. Why do you think they call it Hollywood? It's not real! All of my daughters chose to believe it anyway. They were convinced there were four Noah Calhouns running around this planet somewhere, saving up all his romantic (and completely original) ideas until, one day, he encountered the only love of his life and would be crazy enough to hang from the top of a Ferris wheel to get a date with one of them! (Yes, it's a chick flick, and yes, my girls made me watch it with them.)

Sometimes fathers of daughters may feel, "I've messed up so badly, and if there is a God He definitely can't and wouldn't forgive me." Nothing could be further from the truth. Right now, we need to try to embrace a new mentality: What's in the past is past; now let's take a brand-new step and keep on walking.

Dads, if you have reached your end, when you feel like you have nothing left, maybe it's time to try something new. Maybe it's time to bring a stronger, perfect, 100-percent-satisfaction-guaranteed ingredient into the mix. One who knows exactly where your heart is and what your daughter is feeling. Maybe now is the time to pray with your daughter and thank the Lord that we have unconditional acceptance and love through Him alone. If they won't pray with you, pray for them every single day. I promise, things will change. If you pray faithfully to God and surrender to Him, the pain, anger, and resentment will gradually dissipate. Please don't knock it until you try it, men. Now, you may say, "Silva, I have! And all three times I heard nothing!" May I propose that perhaps, yes, you were saying the words to a prayer, but were you really praying? And praying faithfully? God is not impressed with how nice our prayers sound. He is concerned with our hearts. If you don't know how to pray, talk to Him. If you don't know what to pray, say that. I promise that if you pray faithfully, God will answer. I have documented proof that Almighty God has answered hundreds and hundreds of my prayers!

Next time you see your daughter, look her straight in the eye and say, "I love you just the way you are!" Dads, you know girls. If they have dark hair, they want blonde. If they have short hair, they want long. It doesn't seem to matter how beautiful they were, our daughters always wanted to look like someone else.

Encourage their goals, ambitions, dreams, and personalities. If we don't accept them, love them, hold them, and tell them they are valuable, guess what guy will? Don't be afraid to blow the whistle on what they wear, either. They may wear inappropriate clothes and do strange things to get attention. Believe me, the "wolves" will give it to them. Therefore, we must lavish them with acceptance of who they are today, and all they will become tomorrow.

ACTION STEPS

☑ Swallow your pride. Seek forgiveness, apologize sincerely, and open the door for your daughter to treat you as you have just treated her.

☑ Accept your daughter no matter what! Love her unconditionally. Tell her you believe in her and that you want a relationship with her that lasts a lifetime.

☑ Choose a time in the near future when you can express to her in conversation or on paper that you accept her for who she is today.

What My Dad Just Told Your Dad

by Jenna Silva

Ladies, I don't know about you, but one thing I always longed for and loved growing up was my dad's acceptance—when he told me that he accepted me just the way I was. There were times when I'd pretend I didn't care, or was annoyed with how often he'd say stuff to me. But deep down it would mean the world to me. Today I regret not reciprocating his love and appreciation more often.

Your dad might not be good at telling you how beautiful you are, that he wouldn't want to change a thing about you, or that he would rather have you for a daughter than anyone else. But one day he might start trying. Listen and receive that when he does! As hard as it may be for you to believe, he feels it, so accept it and try to reciprocate. Love and appreciate your differences. Speak kindly even when he doesn't do the same to you, and watch how he'll respond. My dad just shared with your dad that he can never praise you too much, that he should be frequent in lavishing you with words of love. So whether or not you have a dad who has done this, or he's just trying to start now, be open because we are all works in progress.

One of the greatest tools my dad ever got a hold of was the book *The Five Love Languages* by Gary Chapman. Every human being on the planet communicates love in one or more of these "languages." They include: Words of Affirmation, Quality Time, Gifts, Acts of Service, and Physical Touch. This is how my dad found out how my sisters and I differed. For the most part, he shows each of us his love in different ways. He's had to figure out what means the most to us individually and test the five love languages out on each of us to find out for sure. Everyone has a love language. If you don't already know, you should learn your dad's. I encourage you to do one of the following for a week to find out. These are just examples. Try to come up with creative ideas that would mean the most to your father. Drop a few hints if you want him to test it out on you too! Here's some examples:

Monday: Find his favorite TV show or rent a movie and hang out at the house and watch it with him. (My dad's favorite channels are National Geographic and Discovery; for movies he likes anything with action.) Love language: Quality Time.

Tuesday: Write him a note telling him how thankful you are for him, something you appreciate about him, or how much you love him. Love language: Words of Affirmation.

Wednesday: Every time you see him, give him a hug, a kiss on the cheek, sit in his lap like you did when you were a three-year-old in pigtails (trust me, he'll love it), or put your arm around him. Love language: Physical Touch.

Thursday: Make him breakfast in the morning, mow his lawn, wash his car, or go out of your way to do something he needs done (and don't let him pay for it). Love language: Acts of Service.

Friday: Surprise him with his favorite coffee, a gift card to a sporting goods store, a "just because" gift, or a thinking-of-you card. Love language: Gifts.

Listen to him. Hear his heart. He might not always have the right approach or know your love language yet, but be willing to listen anyway. At the core of every girl is the desire to be loved and accepted. As daughters, we would much rather get that from our dads than spend years searching for it in other guys. No one can love us as much as Daddy can. Even if we don't act like it, we want to talk and we long to be accepted. If Dad is willing to listen, it's our job to open up and let him love us.

ACTION STEPS

☑ Discover your dad's love language, and your own.

☑ As females, we desire to have a dad who loves us and lavishes us with attention. However, remember that your dad may not have had the perfect father either. So let's all cut each other some slack! Take the good with the bad, try to let go of the past, and let your dad be a father to you. If you don't, some day you'll wish you had.

"IT KILLS YOU TO SEE THEM (DAUGHTERS) GROW UP. BUT I GUESS IT WOULD KILL YOU QUICKER IF THEY DIDN'T!"

– BARBARA KINGSOLVER

3

OFF THE DEEP END: WAYWARD CHILDREN

I find it fascinating that you can tell a child not to touch a hot stove and seconds later she's screaming in your arms with a throbbing hand, all because of curiosity, disobedience and a driving need to do it "my way."

Our culture praises and encourages independence. Anyone raised in America is likely to declare, "Nobody is going to tell me what to do or how to live. I make my own decisions. I call my own shots." If you are parenting a strong-willed daughter like this—join the club. Ask your daughter(s) why we are here on this earth. For self-pleasure, success, and satisfaction? Then advise them that the moment we begin to prematurely live independently of those over us, we end up screaming out of frustration, pain, and desperation. Men, are we living in dependence on the Lord and modeling obedience, submission, and interdependence on Christ, or setting examples to the contrary? Let me communicate this principle clearly: Our role as spiritual men is to "man up" in every area of life. The only thing God will not hold you responsible for are the things you modeled correctly, yet your daughter chose to rebel against.

Be Her Parent First, and Then Her Friend

One of the most powerful exercises I ever discovered was the time I sincerely asked one of my girls, "Sweetheart, is there anything in my life that I say or do that is wrong, rebellious or hypocritical in any way? If so, I beg the Lord God's forgiveness and yours. If I'm not hindering you, then, sweetheart, if you were to die right now and stand before God Almighty, you alone bear full responsibility for your actions, words, and attitudes. Before God, you will have no one to blame or accuse."

Dads are not into highlighted hair weaves, French manicures, or the movie, *How to Lose a Guy in 10 Days.* We are, however, desperate to connect with our daughters. Some of us have tried to buy her love and deny her no material possession, but we know that doesn't work.

I'm convinced that there is a time in a teenage girl's mind that she does not want or need us to be her friend (first of all, you can't text fast enough to be her friend!) What she longs for is stability, true north, someone she can count on like Jesus Christ, who is the same yesterday, today and forever. Dads, we are to be Jesus with skin on for our daughters. Be her parent first. When the fullness of time has come, she will invite you into her circle of friends.

Integrity is critical for a teenager. In their high school years, I believe our girls see and hear everything. That's why integrity is so important and essential for us to possess. We need to show our daughters *real* love by being a man of our word, caring enough to give her boundaries, never giving up on her, and even gladly laying down our life for her.

That's real love. That kind of love was first displayed when Jesus Christ, God's Son, died on the cross to bridge the gap between sinful man and Holy God.

Avoid the easy road. The easy road is to let her do what she wants, when she wants. We are mandated to love our children always—even when they seem "beyond impossible." Do not be afraid to be the parent and to disappoint, discipline, or stand alone sometimes. Although it's always our first choice to keep our daughter in pigtails, be her hero, and the only man in her life forever. She will grow up way too fast!

Many times I felt like a failure as a father for traveling so much while my girls were growing up. When Crystal would debrief me on who was disrespectful or disobedient, it grieved my heart because she had to discipline and raise them by herself for periods at a time. I used to think, *If only I had an 8 to 5 office job, maybe they wouldn't struggle so much. Maybe their attitudes would be better.* I sometimes wondered if I was in the right line of work.

I tried to communicate and show my love while I was home, but I felt like it wasn't enough at times. Yet for you dads who are fortunate enough to be home every night and communicate what you want whenever you can, do our daughters still rebel? Yes, sometimes they do.

We know that we love our girls, but they must know it too. Dads, actions are critical, but if we don't realize how important our words of affirmation are, it is time to re-evaluate.

A Healthy Way to Honor Her Desire for Freedom

Has your daughter ever put up a fight when you've given her a curfew? Or told her she can't go to Maggie's birthday bash because tonight is family night? I don't know about you, but in these situations I'm sure that "OK, Daddy, I would rather spend time with you anyway" was the furthest thing from her mind. I often think back to certain situations and wonder: What if I would have given her what she wanted? What if I would have let her go to that birthday party or let her spend the night at Cathy or Joanne's house, even though Crystal and I had never even heard of either friend before that night?

Did I hold on too tightly? Was I too strict? My daughters would argue, at least in some cases, I was.

Was it lack of trust? Was it fear of losing her or her getting hurt? Was it the Holy Spirit stirring hesitation in my heart? At one time or another, I'm sure all of these have been true. There are two extremes when it comes to the danger signs in parenting. Either we read too much into everything and make it impossible for our daughter to prove herself and build a foundation of trust. Or, we are so naïve that we end up repeatedly getting "played" by every angle.

Maybe you assume that I have the perfect family—there's nothing we don't talk about, right? Or maybe you think my girls have been perfect and never sinned a day in their lives. That may be true for my bride, Crystal, but unfortunately our four girls take after their father!

I had absolutely no idea what I was doing when we started raising our oldest, Jenna. After all, we got married when I was barely twenty years old. When Delight came along almost three years after Jenna, the process was a bit more familiar but still had its hiccups. Two years after that, I was patting myself on the back, thinking I could parent Grace with my eyes closed. Kristianna came five years later and everything I thought I knew…did not work!

All of them had friends with different circumstances, and yes, guys with different backgrounds. Some of the guys used flattering compliments for Crystal and me. Yet each of the girls had similar stories, whether it was junior high, high school, or even their college years. Each of our girls struggled in her own way. In the midst of it, parenting seemed to hit us like a ton of bricks—they could be perfect princesses one day and a nightmare the next. The dark days seemed to last forever. You might be in the midst of the fire right now, but don't give up. Hold on to hope. This too will pass!

Rebellion doesn't overtake daughters in one swift motion, like a gust of wind. Rather it slowly pulls them down, bit by bit, compromise by compromise. It's as if someone takes a chisel in hand, finds weaknesses (each catered to individual lives), and gradually begins to chip away goodness, joy, purity, peace, self-respect, love, and hope. Until, one day, our daughters wake up and realize that they are completely numb. They have no interest or desire to do anything but please themselves. When this happens, pushback occurs toward anyone who contradicts *how she feels* or *what she wants*. Most kids push away the people they need the most, substituting those who will "join in on the fun." Be on guard, my friend, because it happens to the best of us at one time or another. With our four girls I've experienced several warning signs that have proven to be common denominators:

#1 Wrong Friends

The book of Proverbs continually reminds me of this simple truth, "You become like the people you hang out with." I learned it the hard way growing up, and saw its metamorphosis in my daughters' lives. Looking back, I remember when Kristianna started hanging out with a different crowd. At first we knew all her regular friends that were in her grade; all were very close to one another. But when she joined the high school dance team, she made new friends, many of them older. Crystal and I soon noticed various changes and a hardness about her—subtle at first and then more apparent. And, rather than inviting her new friends to our house, she was spending a lot of time at theirs. Why were we not allowed to meet them? Why would she rather hang out over there than with us? When your daughter begins distancing herself from the friends who have a good background, strong faith, morals and families, pay attention!

Is your daughter extremely private about talking on the phone? Is she skipping classes at school? How does her attitude smell? That's right...smell! When she begins to push back and make up excuses for not going to church or youth group anymore, take note. All of these visible outward changes are signs for parents that something inside of our daughters is agitated, painful, or confused. The solution: fast and pray, and be intentional about spending more time with your daughter. Then fast and pray some more. As Luke 18 instructs, pray and do not quit until you get your answer. Finally, do something fun with her. Take her on a trip; try to get her out of town. We discovered that lifting our daughter out of her environment allowed her to enter ours!

#2 A Double Life

What Daddy doesn't know won't hurt him, right? Wrong! What Daddy doesn't know will hurt everyone involved. Sin will find her out. It will expose her. Eventually, truth always comes out. No matter how good she covers her tracks, the minute she thinks she couldn't possibly get caught...watch out! Depending on personality and how she can get the best reaction that she desires, she may create a hypocritical lifestyle. This life of secrecy and deceit will mean looking, talking, and acting one way with friends, and another way with family.

Why are any of us more likely to go thirty miles per hour over the speed limit on a secluded country road rather than downtown next to the police station? Answer: fear of getting caught. Sin thrives in darkness, secrecy, and seclusion. When you see these "signs," turn on the light! Someone is trying to hide something. For your daughter's own good, you need to know what it is so you can successfully rescue her from it—or him!

#3 Culture Reigns as King

Have you noticed how quickly your little girl has transformed from a princess in pastel turtlenecks to an attention-seeking young woman in plunging necklines and revealing miniskirts? Where did that come from? My observation is that our culture fuels this fire. Magazines like *Us Weekly*, *People*, and *Vogue*. Unending episodes of *America's Next Top Model* and *Extreme Makeover*. Blown-up photos and videos of Britney Spears and the Pussycat Dolls. Our daughters feel insecure because successful media campaigns demand that they do. Our culture puts more value on plastic and silicone than on steel-cut integrity and character.

Every day our daughters feel the need to look like the magazine models who make up, push up, and fill up anything that perks up their self-esteem. Whether your daughter is (in the words of high school culture in the USA) plain, emo, skater, punk, preppy, skimpy, trendy, or tomboy, she's trying to make a statement. She's trying to fit in or stand out. Let her know that she's loved and accepted just the way she is. Focus on the character of her heart more than the fashion of the moment.

Take time with her. Listen to her music (my daughters still can't believe Aerosmith and the Rolling Stones were around when I was in high school!) Talk to her about the kind of movies she likes and why. Is there a coffee shop where she likes to hang out? Go see it. Enter into her world; you may become educated rather quickly!

Where does she put money, emphasis, and value in her life? This is the bottom line. When you understand this, you understand her! Dads, it's our job as fathers to lead by example and to stand up for godly wholesome living, purpose, and direction. Declare war on cultural "norms." Our girls need to know by our example that it is possible to swim upstream, be strong, and stand alone. Talk to your daughter about your successes and failures in this battle!

Grace is given to the humble and strength to the weak. I choose to believe God when He promises He will never lose heart in us. Believe in Him, because He believes in you. Love Him, because He is crazy about you!

Listen: a father-daughter relationship is for life. There is no back door, no way out or easy fix. Our *only* option is success and stick-to-it-tiveness. Hang on to her. Do not let go. Do not turn your back. Do not walk away from her.

She will not always talk to you the way she does now. Her attitude will not go to the grave with her. Remember that you are now different than you once were. Did you catch that? You are older, wiser, more experienced. It takes time to mature, learn, and grow. Dads, give your daughters permission, time, and space as you patiently wait for her to grow into what she was created to be.

ACTION STEPS

☑ Engage. Find out where your daughter puts her money, emphasis and value in life. Understand this and you understand her.

☑ Honor her desire for freedom in a healthy way. However, use your head. Watch for the signs that alert you that something is up. Ask God for wisdom. Why? Because you must respond appropriately.

☑ This week, take your daughter out for a Coke or coffee and remind her that you are aware of the negative pressure she feels. Tell her you believe in her, want to help her make it through this season of life and that you love her. End your time by praying God's blessing upon her life.

What My Dad Just Told Your Dad

by Kristianna Silva Fisher

Why is it that we make so many things feel like a "lose-lose" battle for our dads? You know those times when we can tell he's really trying to say the right thing, do the right thing, be there for us, and yet we just get annoyed at how he's all up in our business? So we push him off and pull back? We can be real brats! Harsh, I know, but we've all done it! I know for my dad, no matter what he would try at times, and how hard he held on, or how often he would tell himself to let go and give me my space, he never seemed to get out of the doghouse and on my priority list for the week. I gave Dad some grief, especially in the high school years. I was continually trying to break free from any "perfect little daughter" label, or the infamous question from acquaintances, "You're Jenna/Delight/Grace's little sister, right?"

If Dad would have ever let me go completely off the deep end, gave me no rules, and let me do whatever I wanted when I wanted, I would have thought he didn't care about me. That he was more consumed with work or my older sisters than with me. But the times when he did hold on tight (at the time, too tight for my liking) made me feel like he was a drill sergeant.

I was so afraid that if I ever told him about my struggles, I would get punishment instead of advice or an hour-long rebuke instead of a hug. He would wonder why I wouldn't talk or open up; it was because I was scared to death of disappointing my parents. I'm a people-pleaser. Even when I had a hard heart I could never live with the feeling of failure for long. I always had to make things right.

Every situation is different, but compromise and respect are absolutely key. When I felt as though Dad didn't even listen or hear me when I'd state my perspective, I got frustrated, agitated, and hard-hearted. I would pull back fast and shut down. Or, at times, out of disrespect and rebellion, I'd fly off the handle. I know now that Dad knew best 99 percent of the time, and he was trying to keep me from making costly mistakes. But there was nothing quite like experiencing things for myself.

Thankfully, though I can still relate to the feeling, my perspective on this has changed. Deep down we all have a rebellious, destructive desire to be in control of our own lives. We yearn to make our own decisions and go down our own path.

Body piercings are common in our culture—nose, ears, lip, tongue, eyebrow, and the infamous belly button. Most of us girls have, at some point, entertained the idea of one somewhere, right?

Dad would say, "Kristianna, why do girls get their belly button pierced?"

"Because it's cute," I'd reply.

"No, be honest," he would say. "Most girls want to pierce their belly button because they want to show it off!" (Ummm. He had me!)

Why be the kind of girl sending a desperate message like that? Why cry out for attention? Why advertise what is not for sale?

Now I understand that all our dads want is to protect us. They want us to make better choices than they did when they were our age!

Of course, I know now without a doubt my dad was the greatest father, prayer warrior and friend. He loved me, even when my reciprocation of that love seemed non-existent. I understand now why he protected me the way that he did, and if he would have just "wiped his hands clean" of me, there is no way I would be loving him like I am today. Yes, he made mistakes, but he never stopped loving me and leading me by his example.

Girls, stop putting unrealistic expectations on broken, imperfect humans (our parents). My dad would often say, "Honey, all I want is for you to treat me with the same respect and concern that you treat your friends with."

We love and need our dads. Let's be thankful that we have them in our lives; many can't say that. The last thing we need is for dads to give up on us.

True or false: Are dads perfect? OK, then true or false: Are daughters?...I rest my case!

ACTION STEPS

☑ Ask your dad to forgive you for that most recent incident. Sign a "peace treaty" with him.

☑ Thank your dad for his wisdom. Remember his goal is to protect you from making the same selfish mistakes he did. He's in your life as your protector and guardian for a reason. (Next, smile and extend your hand to help him up off the floor!)

☑ Let's face it, we will never have every single thing we want (unless we're Oprah)—that's life. We need to get over it and stop throwing a fit when we don't get our own way. The "no's" your dad gives you today will better equip you to handle life tomorrow.

"SOMETIMES, WATCHING YOUR DAUGHTER BEING COLLECTED BY HER DATE FEELS LIKE HANDING OVER A MILLION DOLLAR STRADIVARIUS VIOLIN TO A GORILLA."

-JIM BISHOP

4

RELATIONSHIPS AND YOUR GIRL

No doubt you've heard of the bestselling book, *Men Are from Mars, Women Are from Venus.* Many girls acknowledge that guys are "visual" creatures. So, can anyone explain why they insist on going out in public wearing the smallest, shortest, lowest, tightest clothes possible? All the while playing the innocent card!

What message are we allowing our girls to send these hungry ~~wolves~~ young men? (My editor said "wolves" was too harsh of a word, so I crossed it out!) Some of the lines I've heard my daughters give over the years make me chuckle and want to rip my hair out, all at the same time. Lines like: "What I wear doesn't really make a difference. Guys don't even notice me." (Not true). Or, "So why should I be affected and have to miss out on cute clothes because of the guys' problems?" (A comment that is both naïve and lame).

For girls, relationships are everything. My Grace started dating early. If you can call sitting a foot away from each other in the comfort of my safe lawn a date. Or, walking her to English class. Or, holding her hand while rollerblading up and down the neighborhood block, waiting for his mother to come pick him up before his 7 p.m. curfew.

I'll never forget when Grace was in junior high and we were living in the Chicago suburbs. My angel was a seventh grader. "Stevie" had just entered the sixth grade and recently upgraded from training pants to big-boy boxers. They were always exposed because his string-bean, half-pint body was about six times scrawnier than his pants. I typically thought, "First of all, where is your belt, son? A belt will keep those britches around your waist instead of bouncing off your ankles."

One day, this young man showed up at my home, and I conveniently answered the door. My head immediately dropped from eye level to about 3-foot-11. I believe his words were something like, "Sup. Is Race in?"

I paused a moment trying to process who this boy was, why he did not acknowledge my authority, and what "sup" meant! And by the way, who in the world was "Race?"

Uncharacteristically, I respectfully replied, "Well, son, we are having dinner right now and next time you refer to my daughter as an adverb rather than a noun.... " Just then, Crystal dashed up to the door and said, "Michael, be nice, Honey. Invite the young man in!" Oh brother, I was livid.

Grace, nudging me out of the way, batted her eyes at "Stevie" and shot a glare at me that was worth two words: "Drop dead!"

I walked to the living room window and peered outside at Grace sitting with "Stevie" in the designated spot on my safe, green lawn and watched critically. "Stevie," as I said, was vertically challenged while Grace was a perfect five-foot-five. (Got the picture?) His idea of owning some wheels was his skateboard. His blond bowl cut was, in my opinion, perfect for his prepubescent face. As I watched them, staring at each other after exchanging three lines of conversation, it was painfully apparent that they had nothing in common except for attending the same school and owning a pair of rollerblades.

After a week or so, Grace finally kicked ole "Stevie" to the curb. (Oops, sorry...broke up with him.)

Those years were only the tip of a large, frozen-hard iceberg. My girls have claimed at times that they "had to have a boyfriend." I still don't get it. What for? They had me! We fathers are supposed to be number one in our daughter's lives forever, aren't we? Or is that just a line I've been fed every time one of them wanted the car, cash, or my approval of a prom date?

I heard an excellent illustration years back from a family friend: A girl's life is like a rose. Every time she has a boyfriend, it's like giving a part of herself away. To this guy, here's a petal. To the next guy goes another petal. Then he's history. You get all the way down the road and go through enough guys and give every last petal away and what are you left with? A stem of thorns! Ladies, dads are so up in your grill because we want what's *best* for you.

Fathers, we must empower and encourage our girls to stand apart from the culture. We need to love them, inspire them, and lavish them with words and affection. We need to be models to them by loving our wives and being faithful, selfless, and romantic. The greatest thing a father can do for his daughter is to love her mother.

Most males like intrigue and innocence, something to work for and a goal to attain. Because we know this as men and fathers, it is our job to clue our girls in! We have to tell them how critical and rewarding it is to give the guy something to look forward to, a reason to love her other than her body. Because if a guy sticks through a relationship from first date to wedding night without getting sex, it's proof that he actually cares about who she is, not just what she looks like. What if our daughters saved physical intimacy and sex for marriage and actually found a guy who loved her for her heart? Imagine how rewarding that would be for her. To us as protectors and providers, what a phenomenal feeling for fathers to hand that responsibility over (in the right time) to a man who has honored our girls, honored us, and proven his love through patience.

It is our duty as a dad, whether our girls are eight, eighteen, or twenty-eight, to be a role model, a leader, and an example of what she should be looking for. No, we are not perfect, but we have been placed into this fathering role for a reason. And we need to do everything in our power to build our daughter's self-esteem so that she doesn't feel that she needs to dress or act a certain way to be liked by a young man.

It's All About Commitment

Fathers, let's try an exercise with our daughters this week. Ask your daughter to think about some characteristics of the kind of guy she wants to marry. I asked a room full of females that question at a father-daughter conference a number of years ago. The qualities they listed were: honest, caring, transparent, trustworthy, pure, funny, respectful, responsible, patient, and committed. All of these are excellent.

After my girls did this exercise, I told them a story of when I was engaged to their mother. A seasoned older man said to me, "Son, I've been married for fifty-two years. I've learned that marriage is a whole lot more about commitment than it is about love." My girls laughed at the sight of me in the morning, but it gave me an opportunity to teach them that marriage is much more about commitment than about looks or love. In your marriage, there will be times when you don't feel like loving your spouse; at that moment, you must choose to love.

About ten years ago, two of my nieces attended a father-daughter conference where I asked the girls the question, "What are the qualities you have got to have in the guy you want to marry?" Then I told them, "You know that one of the things that came to your mind is, 'He's got to be hot! He's got to be a looker! I want him to be ripped, rugged, and robust.' But can I ask, is that a 'must have?' Or would you prefer honesty? Would you prefer integrity? Would you prefer faithfulness? I don't want you to write down 'long, curly locks streaming down his back and piercing blue eyes that drill to the depths of my soul.' Use this as a serious exercise and as something you will not back off. Entitle it, 'I'm waiting for…' and put it in a private place. And please do not compromise."

Several years ago my niece Katie got married and I was privileged to perform the wedding. She told me at the rehearsal dinner, "Uncle Mike, remember this list you had us fill out? Remember the 'I'm waiting for…' list?"

"Katie!" I exclaimed with surprise as I suddenly recalled that weekend.

"I want you to know, Uncle Mike, that Jon is every single thing on this list! I did not lower my standards."

I was blown away!

For those dads who have seen the movie *Father of the Bride,* you can understand me. It's the toughest thing in the world. One of my friends told me that when his son got married, he was thrilled. He loves his daughter-in-law, and God bless her for marrying his son. But then he leaned over to me and said, "Silva, when my first daughter got married, it was the hardest thing in the world. I was on the last father-daughter dance with her at the reception, and at the end of the song my baby girl lifted her lips to my ear and said, 'Daddy, you will always be number one in my life.' My knees went weak, the tears started coming, and then I remembered, 'I'm feeling miserable like this and I have to pay for the wedding on top of that!'"

It's Never About Me

One of the greatest verses in the Bible is, "Do nothing out of selfish ambition or vain conceit but in humility consider others better than yourselves." (Phil. 2:3). As much as we like to think we are "good people," we hate being selfless. We thrive off of being self-driven and self-sufficient. We often have a "looking out for #1" mentality. I'm convinced that this is one of the biggest stumbling blocks in relationships today, whether with a mate, friend, or between parent and child. Selfishness will infect a healthy relationship quickly and brutally. It will kill a marriage and destroy a daughter-daddy relationship.

There were times when I begged my girls to talk to Crystal and me. All we wanted to know was what was going on in our kids' lives and to please include us. I remember "coaching" a couple of our daughters with the request that they simply treat us (their parents) with the same kindness they treated their friends. It worked! Note how your daughter can go from depressed to exhilarated in seconds! She's on the phone with a friend: "Hey Amanda! Oh my goodness, no you didn't! But you just met him! No way, you did? Oh, we have got to hang out tonight. He-he-he-he."

All I wanted was for her to communicate with me like she communicated with her friends. I ached for that kind of respect. One of my daughters, if she was meeting with a friend and going to be a minute late, would text or call and say, "I'm so sorry, I'll be there as soon as I can." But when she told me she was coming home and then was late, for some reason I often heard nothing. "Why didn't you call?" I would ask. "Oh, my battery was out on my phone," she would say. Or, "I ran out of minutes." Or, "You had your phone off." Or, "You don't even know how to text."

Honor and respect. "Just treat me as you treat your friends," I would say. The bottom line is if we were all living selfless lives, we wouldn't have problems like brokenness or division. Dads, the stuff we tell our daughters is the stuff we know from experience—oftentimes lessons learned the hard way. Girls, if you live your life in rebellion, you will be miserable. When pride gets in the way, you insist on pushing back against the people who want what's best for you. My adopted grandmother said, "Michael, God wants to mold you, but He will chisel you if He has to." Believe me, it's a tougher way to go!

Dads, tell your daughter she's beautiful. Don't make fun of her. Especially if there is an older son, his sister will be the target no matter what. Do not let him say, "You're going to have *another* piece of that pizza?" That just kills a girl. One of the things our girls want more than anything else is to know that we will step in front of them and "take the bullet." So, fight and protect them no matter what. If we do that in the small areas at home, our daughters will be more likely to listen in the bigger areas. When we say, "I would rather you not do this," they will connect the dots because when we take the bullet at home, they can also expect us to take the bullet outside of the home.

One man hit the nail on the head when he said, "I cannot think of any need in childhood as strong as the need for a father's protection." Men, we've got to protect our girls from their brothers, sisters, friends, and anyone else who would hurt them. Her heart is very fragile right now. Protect it at all costs.

Whether it's protecting her from the lies screaming at her through the megaphone of this culture, or from a four-foot-something boy on a skateboard, being a protector is one of the greatest gifts we can give our daughters.

Let's live our lives in such a way that our daughters seek and choose a man just like her dad.

ACTION STEPS

☑ Lead your daughter by example. Give her a man to look up to. Live your life in such a way that she seeks and chooses a man just like you!

☑ Put your daughter above yourself—prefer her as better than yourself.

☑ Relax and realize that she is not going to spill out every detail of her life to you. And that's OK; think of all the stuff you never told your parents about either!

☑ Don't allow your sons or anyone to talk bad or down to your daughter.

☑ Recognize the pressure this culture puts on your daughter. Promote her for who she is and who she will become!

What My Dad Just Told Your Dad

by Grace Silva Rothrock

I am the daughter who dated the most, including "Stevie" for a week or so in junior high. From there, the boyfriend rate skyrocketed! After all, I was the sister who "loved to love." Romantic. Dreamer. Unrealistic expectations. Yes, 95 percent of girls looking for love in a relationship with a boy do not have a good relationship with their dad. This was never my case, however. I've always had a tight relationship with my dad. Still, there was a deep desire to find my husband. If you feel like you are on the same track, you are not alone. Whether you have a good or bad relationship with your dad, it's normal to have a desire for romantic love from a man and a longing to find your husband. But rather than constantly looking for Mr. Right and settling for the temporary fix of Mr. Right Now, focus on being the best woman you can be so you will attract the kind of man you deserve.

    Our culture is out to steal, kill, and destroy every flourishing love of a young woman. Unreal love, sex, attraction, and pursuit are portrayed in theaters, magazines, and on television. When you're feeding your desires with what our culture has to offer, you develop a greater craving for the things of the world. We need our dads to promote all things countercultural in our lives. We want to be led by example and know how a good man lives. Fathers are still human though, and they will disappoint us at times. But then, we are never going to be perfect daughters either. We could stay at home with Dad occasionally instead of going out with friends. Or, tell him "I love you" twice a day instead of just once. If we can put ourselves in his shoes and understand how hard it must be to let go and let us grow up, then maybe we can do our part in loving him and making a relationship with him a priority in our busy lives.

Growing up, when my dad was simply there for my mom, my sisters, and me, it spoke volumes. His example provided a tangible, visible goal for me. It gave me hope and a standard to live by for myself. I know this wasn't the case for a lot of you. I can't imagine the hurt and pain that comes from not feeling loved or accepted by your father. Still, there are men of all ages around us whom God puts into our lives for a reason. Maybe it's just to be that glimmer of hope and to give us that extra boost of strength to keep holding out for the best. I encourage you to find a man—perhaps an uncle, grandfather, friend's dad, or mentor—and observe him. See how he treats you and other women, and the way he lives. Don't expect perfection, but look for the qualities you want in a man that he possesses. Piece together the qualities you find important in a mate and hold out for those traits.

I initiated one of my past relationships with my parents' knowledge. On paper, this guy passed the checklist. He was a Christian, attractive, and adventurous. But when my parents said they didn't have a peace or feel good about the match, I didn't know what to do. I wrestled and struggled inside, trying to weigh out the good and bad. On the outside I was happy, but knowing my parents didn't approve caused great agitation in my spirit. My parents were honest, consistent, and prayed without ceasing. That's when I made the choice to step into my parents' wisdom—into something my twenty-plus-year-old mind couldn't understand.

The disappointment of ending a relationship didn't lose its sting right away, but love truly does cover a multitude of sins. Today my heart is healed and I have met the man of my dreams—a man I love and my parents, sisters, friends, co-workers, and relatives love. Now I know and can see proof that it was all worth it. My parents weren't perfect and they didn't have a perfect method, but they loved me—and loved me and loved me. That love moved me on and healed my heart.

On the other side of the canyon of youthful emotion, I can see my parents' perspective. Rick Warren writes in *The Purpose Driven Life*, "Obedience unlocks understanding." That statement has become a reality in my life time and time again. Whether or not they are good at expressing it, our fathers love us. They truly do. If your relationship with your dad has been on the rocks, or seemingly nonexistent, it's not too late to make amends. Reconciliation is always within reach. Pay attention if people who love you don't feel good about the guy you are with. I know it sounds like a cliché, but love truly is blind.

If you haven't tried it, pray that you would know how to love your dad and how to meet in the middle. Show him respect. If you are holding anger, bitterness, or resentment against him, or are frustrated with him, pray for him anyway. Pray consistently and I promise that loving him won't be as difficult. If you PUSH—Pray Until Something Happens—you may be surprised at the outcome.

ACTION STEPS

☑ Rather than constantly looking for Mr. Right, focus on being the best woman you can be so you will attract the kind of man you deserve.

☑ Find a man—an uncle, grandfather, friend's dad, or mentor—and observe him. How does he treat you and other women? Don't expect perfection, but look for the qualities you want in a man that he possesses. Then piece together the qualities you find important in a mate. Marriage is more about commitment than love.

☑ Record this phrase and put it somewhere you will regularly see or hear it: Obedience unlocks understanding.

☑ PUSH: Pray Until Something Happens. I don't know who said it, but it's great advice!

> "IT IS NOT FLESH AND BLOOD,
> BUT THE HEART WHICH
> MAKES US FATHERS."
>
> –FRIEDRICH VON SCHILLER

5

BIOLOGICAL VS. STEPFATHER DYNAMIC

The National Stepfamily Resource Center estimates that one of three Americans is now a stepparent, stepchild, stepsibling, or some other member of a stepfamily. More than half of Americans today have been, are now, or will eventually be in one or more step situations during their lives.

Whether it's stepfamilies or single-parent homes, the numbers are now through the roof. Evidence points to the issue of children, particularly girls, struggling to juggle multiple dads. Take this scenario: A girl doesn't live with her biological father, who is only partially involved in her life. She primarily stays with her mother, who is remarried to the man who is now the girl's stepfather. Or, her mother has re-coupled and is living with a man who is taking the physical place of the girl's real father, but socially is clueless when it comes to parenting.

If the girl is fortunate, the new man in her life is loving and caring, longing not to replace or fill her real father's shoes, but wanting to contribute to her life in a positive way and have a thriving relationship with her.

Such is the case for a friend of mine; I'll call him "Sam". His wife has a daughter from a previous marriage, and together they have a daughter and a son. I asked Sam about the ups and downs of parenthood, but I specifically asked him to narrow in on his relationship with his stepdaughter, "Lisa." This is what he said:

What you ask is difficult because I don't think of anything specific when I think about my stepdaughter. Maybe that is important…I never thought of her as anything other than my own. I always wanted Lisa to feel like I was her "real" dad.

One of the more awkward times was when Lisa would go visit her natural father. She would come home and I would feel "diminished," as if I were less important. I think I managed to hide that successfully from her, but it was kind of painful. She would be all pumped up from her visit and begin comparing us. I would feel jealous because he only had to be prepared for a single weekend event, where I had to grind out the day-to-day stuff. There is always plenty of guilt for any parent and there is plenty more available for stepdads. I think I may have used withdrawal as a defensive technique sometimes. I regret that.

On a positive note, I really tried to emphasize the importance of Lisa's birthday with big celebrations, which were meant to show her that her value in life was secure apart from her daddy's identity. I wanted her to know that her being born was important—that it was God's doing and nothing less.

Supporting Lisa's mother was also an important way of showing her how love can span the gaps. Whenever there was awkwardness with [my wife's] former relationship (not that there was frequently), I wanted Lisa to see that the relationship her mother had with me was solid. I think this was significant for [her]. The uniqueness of her situation was also an open door for expressing how special she was. Compassion for her feelings mattered more than our other two kids and I think that is why.

Isn't it fascinating that a good father, or a good stepfather like Sam, oftentimes seems to have little noticeable effect on his daughter, but a bad father has a huge impact? Whether a father's effect is positive or negative, he is one of the biggest driving forces and strongest foundations for self-esteem. If a dad's actions tear down and hurt his girl, then that foundation is sure to crumble beneath her and leave her abandoned and confused.

I personally have experienced what it's like to live in a blended home. My dad died when I was six years old. Ten years later my mother remarried. I am very grateful that she has not lived alone most of her life.

Sadly, my story of growing up without my father is becoming the norm rather than the exception. And, because of divorce or other factors, your daughter may be feeling torn between juggling you and another father figure.

There are so many variables. If a man steps in when a child is one or two years old, that's one thing. If he steps in when the child is sixteen, that's a whole new ball game. Not everybody will fit this mold, and this is not a cookie-cutter recipe for every person. This is, however, how I learned to cope with the challenges of fathering. The same applies all dads, regardless of your particular situation.

First, there is no substitute for prayer. Stop. Did you catch that? Prayer for your relationships is not just a good idea; it is your only option! Not one goal in my entire life has ever come to me apart from prayer. Prayer is no longer on my "to do" list. It is the driving empowering force in my life. Make it yours!

Second, as difficult as it may be, you must have a face-to-face meeting with your daughter or stepdaughter. This meeting can go several directions. For instance, you could share your heart, then wait for a response from your daughter, and vice versa. Or you can get right to the bottom line, saying something like, "Look, I just want you to know that I want to love you and love your mother, and I desire to take care of you and be your coach and mentor even though I'm not your natural birth father. However, I cannot force you to like me or spend time with me. Whenever you are ready, I will be here. And if it takes my entire life to prove to you that I want what is best for you, then I'm willing to wait that time because I am committed to this family and

I'm not going anywhere."

Men, if you approach the sticky situation you may be in with your daughter or stepdaughter with this kind of attitude and tone, I guarantee the truth of those words will penetrate her mind and heart. That will give her the desire to gravitate toward a relationship with you. Be realistic and patient. Things won't be perfect overnight, so don't hold your breath. But this approach will grow her trust with you and she'll come to find she can count on you. One thing you should expect and require from day one in your household is obedience from her and shared respect. It's a two-way street.

If you're a biological father who shares parenting responsibilities with your ex-wife and her new husband, you should have a civil, adult conversation with them. Say something to your ex like, "It is unfortunate that our marriage didn't work out, but I am committed to our children for the rest of my life." And then you can encourage her husband by saying, "When I can't be there for my daughter, she will need you to love her, encourage her, lead her by example, and love and respect her mother." When you talk to your daughter, be sure to tell her the same. And just because there will be two fathers and two different relationships, that doesn't mean that one is more important than the other. So, please don't make her pick a "favorite dad." Both can be appreciated and add to the child's life in a positive way. You may not like the situation and circumstances, but you can learn from every scenario of life.

If you are the child of divorced parents and don't like it, then make a commitment today to never divorce the person you marry. Period. Refuse to put your children in the situation you were or are in. Learn all you can and press on! If what you are facing today troubles you to the core of your being, promise yourself and God Almighty that you will not repeat the pattern. Vow to break the cycle, starting today.

Whatever your story, I think the greatest and most effective remedy for having a positive relationship with your daughter or stepdaughter is to make sure you are being the best dad, mentor, and man you can be for her through fostering a relationship full of mutual respect, admiration, honor, and unconditional love. Do this, and the rest will have room to fall into place.

ACTION STEPS

☑ Commit to the Lord God and those around you not to give up. "So let's not get tired of doing what is good. At just the right time we will reap a harvest of blessing if we don't give up" (Gal. 6:9).

☑ Pray. There is no substitute for prayer.

☑ Be patient and don't expect the dynamic to change overnight.

☑ Two fathers equals two different relationships. It doesn't mean one is more important than the other. Don't make her pick a favorite.

What My Dad Just Told Your Dad

by Kristianna Silva Fisher, featuring an interview with friend "Mary"

One of my dear friends (for the sake of her privacy I'll call her "Mary") was kind enough to open her heart and shed wisdom on her journey through the dynamics of having a biological father and a stepfather, but often feeling like she had no father at all.

I had a stepfather come into my life at a young age. It was hard to understand why a new guy was waltzing into my life, my mom's life, and our home. Change is always hard and uncomfortable. I didn't get to choose who was going to be my dad. Of course, I naturally felt a stronger connection to my biological father. I had some loyalty issues. After living with my stepdad, however, I realized I could make room for both dads...and so can you!

My childhood was not stable. It was extremely insecure and disjointed. I didn't live or grow up in one place. For about eight years, I saw my real dad every other weekend. The time I spent with him wasn't healthy. But it was good. I have fond memories of spending time with him. The dynamic of a father-daughter relationship completely changes when you only see him on the weekends. He's not there to take you to school; he's only there to take you somewhere fun or buy you something.

My relationship with my stepfather wasn't healthy either. The dynamic was really different. It's confusing to know what a good father-daughter relationship looks like unless you have one.

I never called my stepfather "Dad." As I got older, I realized I was open to him taking that role. It's not that I didn't want him as a dad, but he didn't step up to the plate as a father. Every case is different, but a dad has to be a dad before a daughter can be a daughter. A father is the person who defines a daughter. I don't know how to be a daughter to a father because I've never had someone who I've felt has been a real father. To me, that is someone who protects, who I can relax with, and who makes me feel like I don't have to be the strong one. I feel that's what a father should bring to the table. In a father-daughter relationship, the father should lead. Then we, as daughters, take our lead from them!

A dad needs to be the initiator. A lot of this can often translate into dating relationships when you are older, which I'm learning. It takes a lot of work to have a healthy romantic relationship when you didn't have a healthy father-daughter relationship. You learn from your parents about what a healthy father and mother dynamic looks like and what a healthy marriage relationship looks like. I ended up taking a lot of responsibility for what happened [with my father's marriage], so now my tendency is to take responsibility in my dating relationships.

I felt let down and abandoned by both my fathers. My biological father passed away when I was young and I felt so alone! And with my stepfather, I felt abandoned because he never stepped up as a father figure, *despite years of opportunity to do so. I've never fully let myself trust someone for fear of being abandoned and hurt. I'm still overcoming those fears today. I don't know what else to say except, girls, it's OK to feel disappointed and abandoned. However, let's choose to not feel like a victim. It's OK to not be strong and it's OK to be hurt by the absence or failure of a father figure in your life. Do not ignore the problems you face—that can be detrimental in the long run. For many of us, our tendency as women is to not feel hurt or sad. However, you have to let yourself go there so you can move on, get past it, and embrace healthy relationships. I now know they are possible. Just remember, the Lord is our strength!*

Just like Mary has discovered, healthy relationships, between you and your father or stepfather are within reach and possible. Let yourself feel whatever you experience, so that you can move past harboring bitterness and hurt. Break the chains of the past by embracing freedom in your life today.

ACTION STEPS

☑ Make a choice! Remember, you didn't get to choose your dad, but you can choose what kind of relationship you have with him!

☑ Make room for your father and stepfather. Do not compare them.

☑ Talk about your hurts, but don't be a victim of them. Trade your sorrows for the joy of the Lord!

"THE ONLY PROBLEM WITH MY DAUGHTERS IS THAT THEY HAVE TOO MUCH OF ME IN THEM!"

-MIKE SILVA

6

BAD LABELS AND COMMUNICATION

Maybe you grew up in a family with several siblings. Or you may be an only child. Whatever the case may be, you can be sure that people formed assumptions about you—snap judgments.

Track with me for a moment. I was the third of three children with two older sisters. Left without a father at age six, my mother raised me. I got married when I was exactly one month out of my teens, and now I have four adult daughters. My dog is female. My entire house smells and looks feminine. "Pink" is everywhere. (FYI, my mother has ten granddaughters and no grandsons!) Now that several daughters are married, I'm not the token male anymore. My sons-in-law are men's men. Outdoorsy. Car guys. Woodworkers. Hikers. Meat eaters. (Grunt with me, dads!)

What I just wrote about my sons-in-law is an example of the labels we attach to people. Labels are everywhere. We use them constantly. Some are good, but many of them are damaging, specifically as it relates to our daughters. Fat. Nerdy. Bookworm. Teacher's pet. Boring. Awkward. String bean. Chatty Cathy.

Labels are used to describe people on the street, a teacher, a co-worker, a grandparent, a crazy aunt, or other family members. In grade school the kids called me "Sylvia" or "Saliva."

When my girls were growing up, I had preconceived ideas of who they were going to be. Oftentimes, I treated them according to their birth order. Even worse, I would use the same parenting tactics that birthed "results" in one daughter on another. This often came back to bite me in the "hind parts!"

Let me explain. Jenna has always been my "buddy." She went to the garbage dump with me and ran errands with me to the hardware store and car wash. In her younger years, we played sports together and enjoyed quality time with each other. That's how I showed her I loved her. When I needed to discipline her, taking away her social network— no hanging out with friends, no television—would usually help her shape up more quickly than anything else. If we tried to sit her down in a corner and give her a time-out, she would figure out a way to have fun in the corner!

I tried the same tactics with Delight. However, her likes and dislikes were totally different. When Delight got in trouble, I reverted to what had worked with Jenna—taking away social time or banning the TV until she got her grades up again. That didn't work. The best way to communicate with Delight was sitting her down and instructing her about what she did wrong and explain how to make it right. Delight was a perfectionist who would rather have had her wisdom teeth pulled without sedation than hurt or disappoint those she loved. If she ever sensed we were disappointed with her, it crushed her.

The younger two had different ways to communicate and conquer the labels we assigned to them. For sensitive Gracie, one look at her with an unhappy glare and she would shape up so fast I could have gotten serious whiplash! Kristianna thrived on attention and love. She wanted to be with us—especially her sisters. A scowl of correction didn't work with Kristianna. If we told her "no" to staying up past her bedtime or kept her home with her mother and me instead of allowing an activity with friends or sisters, she would be devastated and do whatever it took to make things right.

As you have likely discovered, every daughter beats to her own drum. To avoid damaging our relationships with them, it's important for fathers to learn the most positive way to communicate effectively with them.

As fathers, we need to do all we can to keep the peace with our girls. Nothing is worth broken relationships. Drill that truth into your daughter's mind. Home is a safe place, and family love and unity trumps all.

Men, fight for your family time together. (This concept is foreign in our society today. Why? Because it is absent in our culture!) As coaches of our households, we've got to stand up against the damaging effects of cultural fragmentation and destructive labels before they destroy fragile hearts.

ACTION STEPS

☑ Family labels are allowed only if they inspire and empower! Write a new label for each child here.

_____

☑ List two ways that your family fights for unity.

    1.

    2.

What My Dad Just Told Your Dad

by Delight Silva Abbott

Goody-two-shoes. Dad and Mom's favorite. The good one. I wore these labels from a young age and used to laugh them off, knowing they were accurate descriptions but not wanting to admit it. I was more responsible than my sisters growing up (but don't remind them of that). When Mom and Dad would leave us alone, they would say to my older sister, "Jenna, you're in charge. Take care of your sisters and no fighting!" Then just before leaving they would pull me aside and say, "Delight, you're in charge. Make sure your sisters don't fight, and when we get back you can tell us everything." So I took this as my obligation—my duty. I wasn't being a tattletale or ratting on my sisters, just obeying Mom and Dad. Pleasing them. I wasn't good at much growing up, so being dad and mom's helper (better known by my sisters as a "tattletale") gave me a sense of pride. I excelled at something.

Over the years, however, the labels and responsibility began to weigh heavily on me. Being a ministry family, we've always lived in a "glass house" with the world (and the church for that matter) looking in, watching our every move and sticking their own labels on us. I can't tell you how many times we heard, "I bet you girls never fight," or "What's it like being so perfect?" or "You Silvas have it all together, don't you?" Those labels couldn't have been further from the truth!

By the time college had come and gone, I harbored a secret pride and bitterness in my heart, although I didn't recognize it at the time. Pride because in my early twenties, I hadn't made the relationship mistakes nearly all my friends had (and I'm just talking about my Christian friends). Nor did I have other major regrets like they did. I can't tell you how much the enemy just loves to make us think more highly of ourselves than we ought! The bitterness stemmed from the labels hung around my neck that I so badly wanted to shed. Now please understand it's not that I wanted to be rebellious or wayward. I was just tired of trying to live up to perfection!

While sitting in her college dorm room one night, I remember one of my friends saying, "Delight, you just don't understand what I'm going through." She was right! I found myself passing judgment on her for something I had never experienced. Because I saw things so black and white, I expected others to as well. I'm sorry to say that was a label I created all by myself! For me, it was the difference between right or wrong, black or white. There was no gray in my world. You see, what started off being just a label turned into pride and bitterness, which the enemy used in negative ways.

I didn't date growing up. I never really knew why, except that I was being protected from something (maybe myself) because—well, let's just say I definitely had an appreciation for the opposite sex! I was the daughter who liked any good-looking male in nice jeans, and wasn't afraid to admit it.

Like any other girl, I dreamed of finding Prince Charming and falling in love. I used to say, "Oh God, I pray that my first boyfriend would be the one! I don't want to date someone unless he's the one I'm going to marry." Similar to many of you girls reading this book, I had high expectations of what it would be like to fall in love.

I didn't have my first real boyfriend until my early twenties. He grew up in a good home with a family similar to mine. I quickly labeled him as "Mr. Right" because he had all the right "ingredients." However, I eventually learned that he struggled to find passion and clear direction in his life. Despite my best efforts to help him, I couldn't. After a lot of painful fighting in my heart and several tough conversations, the relationship ended. I remember thinking that was the hardest thing I had ever done! I mean, I really liked this guy; after all, he was my first love. Everyone remembers their first love, right? I had a hard time letting go, but ultimately I could not ignore that quiet voice of the Lord saying, "Delight, he is good, but I have greater for you. Choose the greater over the good."

It took me a long time to get over that breakup. Afterwards, I remember thinking, "Man, maybe I need to lighten up on guys and give them a chance. After all, I don't want to be single the rest of my life." I allowed doubt and lies of the enemy to establish a foothold in my heart.

Boyfriend number two I labeled "good enough." Being the family's goody-two-shoes and a "Miss Fix-it," I wanted to finally give someone "less fortunate" a chance. I knew he wasn't the type of guy I had been waiting for all my life. Still, I figured that after being around my family and with a little mentoring from my dad, he would be good enough. Right? Wrong. Our relationship ended after a few short months. The Lord had gotten my attention once again and provided the grace I needed to make the right decision.

Boyfriend number three was different from the other two. He had most of the things on my list of non-negotiables. I remember thinking, "Now this is it!" However, "Mr. Perfect" broke my heart, which left me confused, discouraged, hurt, and depressed.

I will spare you all the painful details but I will say that the road that followed (although bumpy and full of tears) led me to healing and restoration. I have learned that it's not the labels that make me who I am; it's the Lord in me! By His blood and His grace we can all wear the labels: *loved, redeemed, forgiven*! I'm so thankful for that. Aren't you?

It should encourage you to know that I did finally find my Prince Charming. By choice, I have now claimed a new label: "Mrs. Delight Abbott." It is one I am proud to bear forever!

ACTION STEPS

☑ Communicate. Has your family placed a label on you that has hurt you or left you feeling bitter? Don't keep quiet. Share your heart with your parents and ask them to help you resolve any negative labels that hurt you.

☑ Refuse situations that you know are wrong. Are you compromising your standards? Ask the Lord to help you make the right decisions! It's one thing to fall; it's another not to get up!

"A WILD GOOSE NEVER LAYS A TAME EGG."

—C.H. SPURGEON

7

MYTH BUSTERS: FACT & FICTION ABOUT DADS AND DAUGHTERS

Kristianna went to several school dances in high school. Every time another one rolled around she would tell her mother, "I need to get a new dress. I really hope someone good asks me to the dance so I don't have to go with a member of the chess team…if you know what I mean."

I remember wandering into the kitchen once where Kristianna and Crystal were brainstorming potential styles and colors and saying,

"Sweetheart, just borrow a dress from one of your sisters or girl friends. Don't think another thing about needing a date. Daddy will take you to the dance. If you want, we can even stop for dinner on the way."

She chuckled, hugged me, and said, "Thanks, but no thanks."

Later that night, I looked at Crystal and said, "Why does she need some 'nasty ole boy' to take her to the dance when she could stay home with her daddy?"

My bride smiled and replied, "Yes, she has you, honey, but you need to stop picturing her in pigtails, thinking she'll want to go to Chuck-E-Cheese for dinner and dance on your feet all night. She's bound to fall in love, just like I did with you. We've got to start bracing ourselves now." (By the way, I hate the movie, *Father of the Bride*. It's depressing!)

With that remark, I reclined in my chair and pouted because I knew Crystal was right. She had just busted a myth I had wanted to believe, that my love would be all that my girls would ever need. It was only the first of many to fail. To review some of the leading ones:

#1: **My Love Is Enough**

Obviously, my precious angel just doesn't understand that I can make her laugh. I can hug her, protect her, and love her unconditionally. So why should she be wasting her time with some Joe Schmo at the school dance? She doesn't need *him*... she has me!

My girls were so sweet to try to ease the sting of shift in affection by telling me, "Daddy, you're still my number one man." Or, "Dad, don't worry. He's still second-best to you."

As much as I loved hearing that (and always liked pretending it was true), I now know that I'm no longer "the man." Besides, fathers would go slightly insane and broke if our daughters remained under our umbrella forever!

Thankfully, the young men entering our family now are better than I will ever be. If you're reading this book, you've probably traveled a rocky road with your daughter and are trying to find some smooth water to get you back on track. Take it from me, it is so easy to be overprotective and "territorial" of our little girls. Be careful, though. Because you are trying so hard to hold on to her, you could push her away. The Aussies say it this way: "The boomerang always returns to the hand that lets it go!"

When the right young man comes into the picture, he won't steal our daughters away from us. He will be an improvement to her life and your family. Hopefully he will fill in the gaps of her weaknesses and shine a light on her strengths. That sounds like a good deal, doesn't it? If it's our job as dads to want what's best for our girls, a man who will make her a better person is best for her. If my precious in-laws (both in heaven now) had insisted that a perfect man marry their Crystal, I would still be single!

Just think, between you and "mystery man," she'll have everything she's ever wanted and all she'll ever need. Let your daughter know she doesn't have to pick you or him—she deserves you both!

#2: Parent Vs. Friend: Pick One

While my girls were growing up, I definitely took a more parental, discipline-based approach. Now that they are adults, I consider them some of my best friends, next to my bride, Crystal. You are not going to be perfect. You won't feel fully confident with every decision you make, nor will your daughter be fully satisfied with your decisions. Still, do the best you can. Love her, listen to her, and lead her by looking out for her best interests.

If you feel like you've driven a wedge between you and your daughter, it's not too late to work on your friendship. Men, hear me. It's never too late! If you feel convicted that you need to step it up as a father, start today. Don't let yesterday's mistakes hold you back. Don't worry about tomorrow because it's never guaranteed. We are only responsible for today. This moment. Now is our time. Regardless of your past, you have a choice to make today that will help shape your relationship with your daughter in the future. To paraphrase Philippians 3:13: "Forget the past. What's done is done. Let it go and press forward." Always move forward!

#3: If You Are the Right Model, She Makes the Right Choice

It's bound to happen. For a while we can use the "She's not allowed to date; she's too young" excuse, or simply not say anything, cock a rifle, and walk out on the front porch (I actually did this for Kristianna. It was great...I thought). The last thing I need is to watch *America's Most Wanted* and see Joe Jr.'s mug shot pop up and realize I have no way to find out exactly where my baby girl is! Not happening. Not on my watch!

In the beginning of the movie, *My Big Fat Greek Wedding*, the main character, Toula, is almost thirty years old. Her entire family is obnoxiously making fun of her for seldom dating and not being married yet, and forcing her to go on dates. You can imagine how that would make any woman feel.

Rather than insisting they find a man, my prayer was that I would be the best example possible for my daughters, and by some miracle they would overlook my flaws and see qualities in me that they desire in a spouse. However, I've discovered that is not always guaranteed. I've talked to many fathers who say, "I'm being a good example to her and she still picks this loser! How is that possible? I don't get it!" I don't yet have the answer to that tough question, but I do know this: continue to pray. Continue to have an open mind and heart. Continue to protect and fight for her when she is not wise enough to protect herself.

In my case, I'm so thankful that it's all good for the moment, but I know for many of you your girls are living with a guy you can't stand. Or she's already married to a man who not only doesn't respect you but doesn't treat your daughter the way you think he should. If this is your story, your daughter needs you now more than ever. As impossible as you think it may be, try to hold on and be engaged in her life. Do not hold this one mistake over her for the rest of her life. If you do, both of you will eventually die with regrets. Furthermore, how will your daughter know how to forgive if you don't show her? You can love her and not like her choices. I love the closing line in

Gregory E. Lang's book, *Why a Daughter Needs a Dad:* "A daughter needs a dad because without him she will have less in her life than she deserves."

#4: Fathers Raise Sons, Mothers Raise Daughters

Your daughter needs you just as badly as she needs her mother, if not more. Nearly a third of children in America live with one parent—usually their mother. *Time* magazine reports, "On every single significant outcome related to short-term well-being and long-term success, children from intact, two-parent families outperform those from single-parent households" (www.Time.com, July 2, 2009). It is for this reason the Scripture says, "And become... kind to one another, tenderhearted (compassionate, understanding, loving-hearted), forgiving one another [readily and freely], as God in Christ forgave you" (Eph. 4:32, AMP.)

The same *Time* article reports that few things hamper a child as much as not having a father in the home. Maria Kefalas, a sociologist who studies marriage and family issues, says that growing up without a father has a deep psychological effect on a child. "The mom may not need that man, but her children still do," Kefalas says.

This truth is seen in the case of a girl named Beth, who found out she was pregnant. Though ashamed and embarrassed, she desperately wanted her parents to hear her side of the story. Fearing the worst, she hid it from them for four torturous weeks. She considered abortion, but knew better. She would rather live with all the consequences that would be a part of her life than make one quick, quiet decision that would haunt her forever.

On the brink of divorce, her mother was an unhappy, unhealthy workaholic who barely gave her daughter sufficient time to talk. Her father was worse. He had lost his job after a back injury two years prior to this. Shortly after that, Beth's brother lost his life in a car accident. Ever since the accident, her father had displayed anger and become even more disconnected and uninterested in his daughter's life.

When she told her parents the truth, her mom exploded with anger and stormed off to work again. Her dad walked into the kitchen, grabbed some liquor, and sat down in his chair without saying a word. Beth tried to get him to open up and help, but he didn't give her a glance of acknowledgement. She needed her father's protection, unconditional love, and full support. Unable to find it, that night Beth ran away. How tragic. One of our roles as dads is to assist our girls in carrying life's burdens that, if left to themselves, will break their back.

#5: She Doesn't Need My Time if I'm Giving Her My Wallet

I can't tell you how many men I've talked to who travel a lot for work or spend long hours at the office who have adopted the idea that parenting is making sure they recharge their daughter's credit card every month. Listen up men, mochas from Starbucks or new cars are not the answer. A free ride through life may buy you some time, but in the process bankrupt your daughter's character.

You might be thinking, "Silva, if I ever tried to switch things up now, she would flip out and push me away."

Dads, trust me on this; she's not going to know which red pumps you bought her four years ago, but she will remember your presence in her life. Tell her she is beautiful and that you love her. Make time to be engaged in her life. If you have enabled her negative behavior, fix it! The rewards of this kind of corrective action will give back to you and your grandkids. Your decision will be liberating. She will know you are there for guidance when she needs it.

#6: What Our Relationship Is Like Today Is the Way It's Always Going to Be

I am thankful this idea turned out to be a myth. If my relationship with my girls was the same as it used to be, I'd go crazy. If I were even still alive! I remember the fights. The screaming. The glares. The anger boiling up in her eyes. My blood pressure shooting through the roof. Waiting up until early hours of the morning, waiting for her to come home and worrying about her. At that age, kids typically only think about themselves, their agenda, and what makes them happy. They completely disregard other parties involved in the situation.

I know you can relate. Whether your daughter is well-behaved and close to you, or she's jumped off the deep end and completely rejected your help, it's built into a father to carry a burden for his daughter's well-being, protection and heart. Don't get me wrong; I'm not saying we are to control her, but we are to watch out for her. There's a fine line, but it's worth taking time to figure out. Don't be okay with a mundane, apathetic relationship. Don't place all the blame on her, even if you strongly feel that's the case. Every father-daughter relationship is different, so it's hard to go off solely my experience. Still, men, we must not settle for complacency and letting our relationships with our girls stay on the back burner. Too often I hear such statements as, "My daughter doesn't want to change," or "Even though I'm willing, she's not, so what's the use?"

If every player on a football team gave up and quit the second he felt his teammate wasn't giving 100 percent, the game of football as we know it would cease to exist. So if you asked me what you should do if your girl isn't willing to meet you halfway, I would reply, "Then meet her 100 percent of the way." Why? Because you are the parent and she is the child. And, ultimately, because she's worth it. If we don't model what we want her character to be, who will? Her friends? The media? Is that what you want?

#7: Of Course She Knows I Love Her...Her Mom Tells Her I Do

Never assume this statement is true. What is true is that mothers are often more verbally expressive and affectionate than fathers toward their children. Dad, this is quite likely an area that demands your attention.

The bottom line is that every daughter aches to be loved by her daddy. Even if Words of Affirmation are not your love language, your daughter still needs them. If you aren't the greatest or most gifted verbal communicator, ask your daughter to help you express what you feel toward her but can't communicate clearly. I guarantee she will love the exercise!

On behalf of all of us who have grown up without the privileged presence of a father, I beg you: Bless your daughters while you can. Affirm them. Believe in them. Love them. Overlook their youthful mistakes. The absence of a father's blessing could haunt her all the days of her life! Think about this, if you don't give her your blessing, where will it come from? If you don't give it, she will *never* benefit from it.

ACTION STEPS

☑ Refuse to allow yesterday's mistakes to hold you back from doing what is right today.

☑ Forgive first. How will your daughter know how to forgive if you don't show her?

☑ Ask for help. Ask your daughter to help you verbalize what you feel toward her but can't communicate clearly. I guarantee that she will love the exercise!

"A DAD'S PRIMARY UNDERLYING JOB IS NOT CONTROL. IT'S TO VALIDATE EVERY ONE OF HIS CHILDREN."

-TIM SANFORD

8

16 LIFE SAVING STEPS

If I were reading this book instead of writing it, at this point I'd be thinking, "Silva, I get what you're saying. You have four daughters—sure you know a little and I can relate to some things you are saying. But I still have more questions. Where do I go from here? How do I get to the place you are talking about? This father-daughter bliss seems so foreign. It's like an impossible hurdle to jump. How do I get from point A to point B? How do I rebuild the relationship with my daughter on a day-to-day basis?"

After thirty-one years of parenting, talking to friends who have daughters, and doing my research, I have compiled a list of sixteen practical steps that you can start today. I guarantee they will take you a long way if you are genuine and consistent with your effort. Here's the good news. All you have to do is remember what this book is about and you are on your way to memorizing ways to boost the FATHER-DAUGHTER relationship!

Follow Through on Promises

The way we build trust with our daughters is by making and keeping promises. If you commit to take her out on a date, let *nothing* get in the way. If you tell her you are coming to her dance recital, *make sure* you are there. If you promise to keep a confidence, don't share it with others. Her seeing you follow through on your commitments will build your relationship. It will also let her expect other men in her life to be trustworthy.

Activities Are Key

Make time for fun! If you have a younger daughter, take her to look at toys at the toy store and then out for a treat. If she is a little older, take her to see a movie or to her favorite store and buy her a shirt she's been wanting. Go for a casual walk or a hike, or go camping if she likes doing that. If she's an adult out on her own, set up a time to get together and make dinner, play games, walk around the park, or attend a professional sporting event. Consider playing miniature golf, swimming, seeing a play, or going to a comedy club (after making sure the comic is family-friendly). Doing things you both enjoy builds memories. Spending time having fun with our girls means the world to them. If all we do is scold them, punish them, fight with them, or barely notice them because we are tired from a full day of work, boredom and frustration are sure to settle in.

Take Time to Listen

Many of our daughters love to talk (can I get an "amen?") In my experience, girls tend to vocalize more than boys. What a dad can do to build his relationship with his daughter is to listen more. Pay attention to what she says when you are together. Listen to what she is thinking, dreaming about, and wishing for her life. When she shares something with you that is private and bares her soul, don't repeat the story. Violating her trust is one sure way to damage your relationship. Sometimes what will mean the most to her is sitting and simply saying nothing, but allowing her to know that you are there for her and you care about her.

Help Her Learn New Things

While it's great when a dad teaches his daughter to ride a bike or to read, sometimes the best things he can teach her are "guy things." Skills like changing the oil in a car, fishing, golfing, or home repairs will serve a girl just as well as a boy and give her confidence that she can tackle anything. Just being with her dad doing things he is good at will be a treat for her and will make her a better person in the long haul.

Encourage Her—Tell Her She's Beautiful

This will sound a little corny to some fathers, but it is very important. Modern culture and the media often give our girls messages that they need to be the right weight, wear the right makeup, and dress stylishly—sometimes immodestly—to be beautiful. This was one of the leading recurring topics in my household and one that I feel strongly about. When you tell your daughter she is beautiful, intelligent, respected, a success, a wonderful person, is perfect just the way she is, and that you wouldn't change one thing about her if you could, it means more than you can imagine. Emphasize her beauty on the inside as well as outside—it's important that she realizes beauty is so much more than skin-deep.

Read Together

Anything and everything—let her pick the material, whether a *Vogue* magazine article, a history book, or a novel. It's a great way to spend quality time together. Life is busy, so you may not be able to do this every week. Still, the more time you read with her, the more opportunities you will have for conversation. (I didn't do this nearly enough with my girls.) If I could do it over, I would let them pick something and just sit with them and listen to them read, look through a magazine together, or read to them. It's a great way to spend meaningful, beneficial time with your daughter.

Say What You Feel

I'm not suggesting you have to embrace daisies and roses, but I am encouraging you to talk with her, write to her, go get a coffee, or otherwise get out of the house and turn off *both* of your phones. See what happens! Whether or not your girl takes after you in her impeccable verbal communication skills, every girl of every age loves to be loved and loves to be lavished with nice words and thoughtful statements. You can write on post-it notes or leave a voice mail telling her you are thinking about her and that you are grateful for her. Watch out, though; she may save the message and listen to it over and over again.

Date Your Daughter

Take her out for ice cream, dinner, or a movie. Let her browse her favorite store. Attend a sporting event or go bowling, or do whatever she likes to do. Let this be a time to laugh and hang out. You will have fun seeing her have fun. Taking your daughter on regular dates is a great way to stay connected. This one-on-one interaction will always be time that you cherish and she will remember.

A Little Touch

Hugs, goodnight kisses on the cheek, holding her hand, piggyback rides, sitting on your lap—our girls need to feel our love, not just hear about it. Sometimes fathers are a little standoffish with daughters, especially a father who has sons. We are naturally more comfortable doing guy stuff, but it's important to give daughters our attention and appropriate affection.

Understand Her Perspective by Listening

Listening is a key in any relationship, but I would argue it's most important in your relationship with your wife and daughter. That's why I need to hit this topic again. One thing I've learned is that girls need you to listen to them more than they need to hear what you have to say. Remember gentlemen, men love to fix things. If you don't want me to fix what's broken, then don't ask my opinion, right? Now that's perfectly logical thinking for a male! But it does not fly with females. I've tried!

Try listening without judging or offering advice. Sounds easy, but trust me, it takes intentional effort. She truly does desire for you to simply sit and listen to her share thoughts without saying anything in return. She wants an ally. She wants a safe sounding board off which to bounce thoughts and ideas. Reflective listening is an important skill for fathers to develop. Your daughter will really appreciate your focused efforts to listen.

Get Involved in Her Interests

If your daughter is into soccer, offer to coach the team, or at least go to practices and games with her. If she is taking music lessons, listen to her practice and go to recitals. Compliment her on her involvement in her interests, hobbies, and diversions, whatever they may be. Learn something about her interests so you can talk about it with her and help her excel. My girls have been interested in everything from softball to basketball, cheerleading, choir, dance, traveling, art, and music. Name it and it's probably been an interest at some point in our household. It's good and healthy for your girls to dream, compete, and experiment so they can sort out what they truly enjoy for the long term, versus what they only want for a season. They will welcome your encouragement and participation.

Her Friends Matter

Spend time with her and her friends. Try to connect with those closest to her. If you've ever wondered what in the world your daughter is thinking...ask her friends! I guarantee you they will know. Particularly in adolescence through high school and college years, your daughter's friends will become an extremely important part of her life. She is like clay—she'll be shaped and formed by whatever or whoever she is around the most, be that positive or negative. She will tell her friends things that she won't tell you or her mother. Make sure you know who her friends are. Host a few parties or sleepovers at your place so you can get to know them better, or simply be present when they are around. Caution: Do not breathe down your daughter's neck or try to be "too cool" because that will turn her off. (That's experience talking!)

The Crossroads Count

Be there during the critical moments in her life—birthdays, first day of school, first date, first dance, first prom, engagement, wedding, and the birth of children. These are road marks she will remember forever. I was traveling so much for work that I missed some important days, but if it was at all possible, I was there. Men, our families—our girls—always take top priority over our jobs. We may forget that we missed an important event, but she won't.

Exemplify Manhood—She's Watching

The way your daughter sees you treat your wife or your mother makes a huge difference in how she will see men later in her life. Be on your best behavior with her, her mother, and other female friends and relatives. Simple courtesy and kindness will go a long way in helping her know what to expect of men. One of the worst habits in the world is to discredit or degrade your wife or daughter in public. Men, I know very little about very little, but on this particular topic…I am king! Influence your daughter's mind in such a way that she will recognize the caliber of man she deserves and the kind of guy you want her to associate with. You want your daughter's mentality to be, "I don't want to settle for any guy that doesn't match up to how great my dad is!"

Respect Her Mom

This may be out of your control, as you may no longer see or communicate with your daughter's mother. If you do, however, it is very important to respect her. If you demean her mother or make her mother seem smaller and less significant in your daughter's life, you are indirectly putting a wedge between you and your daughter. If you are still married to her mother, it's even more of a platform to be a great example. Sometimes, we treat our children the same way we treat our spouses. We may feel like this is different. We may not mean to take out our anger and frustrations with our wives on our children, but it does indeed happen. Girls love their daddies, but their moms play a critical role in their lives. When you love your wife, take care of her, protect her, provide for her, and put her needs and desires before your own, you are modeling for your daughter the quality of man she deserves and should seek.

Start Fresh

Every one of us must remember this: no one is perfect. We all make mistakes. There are days when we will say something we shouldn't have, deal with a situation poorly, or just want a "redo" with our girls. That's life. A friend of mine says, "Some days I'm the pigeon; other days I'm the statue!" A clean slate. A fresh start. Another opportunity. That's what we need and desire right? Well, good news…consider this moment as that opportunity. You can begin today putting these practical steps into action. You won't be able to do all sixteen of these at once; many of these suggestions are things you'll need to practice to build trust and a positive reputation. They need to become a lifestyle. I don't want to mislead you—a lot of these things will seem unnatural and difficult. But I promise you they work. Strive for consistency. Be patient; it will take a little longer than you would like to break down the walls of her heart. But the walls will crumble. They have for me!

What My Dad Just Told Your Dad

by Kristianna Silva Fisher

Ever since I was little, I've been asked, "Are you a momma's girl or a daddy's girl?" For a while, I thought the answer was simple: I felt closer to my mom. Perhaps it was because Dad traveled so much, or maybe I was like many girls who went through a phase of feeling more attached to mom and having more in common with her. Thankfully, as I got a little older and with Dad consistently giving me the attention I craved and the love I longed for, my heart shifted to happily embracing the role of daddy's girl.

No matter what connection (or lack of) you share with your father today, I challenge you to remember the acronym DADDY'S GIRL. It will help you memorize some wonderful and practical ways that you can improve your relationship. You may be thinking that your dad is the polar opposite of mine. Nevertheless, I'll step out on a limb and tell you that I believe all ten of these steps will reap vast rewards. Don't expect it to work magically overnight, especially if you are trying to patch up a wound that has been open and sore for a long time. But if you start applying these steps one day at a time and put forth maximum effort, I guarantee there will be huge improvements and everlasting benefits. Give them a try and get ready for results!

Daily Decision

Everyone has a character trait or two that turns people off. There are sure to be things you like and dislike about your dad. Whatever you dislike, you must look past it and decide daily to be a loving daughter without expecting anything in return. It may take longer than you want, but it will pay dividends. Learning to live, love, and follow your dad today prepares you to one day do the same with your husband.

Ask Him Questions

Your dad has more life experience than you do; he has "been there, done that." More time alive means more mistakes, which means more lessons learned. Try asking him questions about life in general. That may help you deal with problems at school or at work. There's a lot you can learn, and a good chance he would love to teach you if you are willing to listen.

Don't Forget the Golden Rule

Do unto Daddy as you would have Daddy do unto you! It works both ways. Do you want him to trust you? Trust him. Do you long for him to affirm you? Affirm him. Do you desire his loving approval and life giving forgiveness? You know what to do!

Discuss

Talk about things, whether it's about your day, school, his job, news on television, life events, or family members. Ask him for his advice. Open communication with his daughter will mean the world to him.

Yourself Second

It's easy to get consumed with your own life, schedule, friends, and activities. When that happens, your relationship with "good ole dad" can fall through the cracks. Be honest: don't you think more about "me, myself, and I" than anyone else? The dictionary calls that behavior SELF-ish! Show your dad you care about him, his interests, and his burdens. See what happens! Would you like it if your father was so wrapped up in himself that he ignored you? I thought so! As I said earlier, "Do unto Daddy as you would have Daddy do unto you!"

Say What You Feel

Your dad is a male, which means he can't read your mind or ever figure you out. Therefore, tell him exactly what you feel. How is it supposed to get better if you are the only one who knows what's wrong? I promise your dad would rather know the truth and what you really think than for you to remain cut off and quiet. Tell your dad you love, need, and desire a close relationship with him. I guarantee he will love it! I know mine does!

Give Your Dad the Same Attention

Invest time and build trust and confidence with your dad in the same way you do with your friends. Respect him and be willing to rearrange your schedule occasionally to hang out with him. You may think that's bad for your reputation or that you are the only girl who voluntarily hangs out with her father, but someday you are going to wish you had put forth more effort. Don't flush precious time that you could have with him because you are so engulfed in your own world.

Imagine Life Without Your Dad

Some of you girls are reading this book together with your dad; some of you are reading it because your mom or dad is making you. Others are reading it because you need to find some sort of hope. You may think your relationship with your father couldn't get any worse. A book like this will either do nothing for your relationship or give you some direction. You may discover where to go from here and how to work on recovering your relationship.

Picture for a moment what your life would be like without your father. Your dad loves you and cares for you. I'm sure he is a work in progress, but we all are, so give him a chance. Learn to appreciate him in your life in spite of the difficulties between you. I would much rather have a father's presence in my life than not. I'll be the first to admit that it's time we girls started to be thankful for what we have and work hard to improve it.

Respect Your Dad

Why? Because there is not another person on the planet who can prepare you for the future as well as he can.

Think about this: could it be that your dad craves your respect so deeply that he is not able to love you properly? What if you respect and honor him so profoundly that he responds with abundant love? Wouldn't that be sweet?

Laugh with Him and Love Him No Matter What

We have no idea how much joy we bring to our daddies. They live to see us smile. They long to have a relationship with us. You should see my dad's face when I show up! He loves me. And I get to love him back! Billy Graham said, "A good father is one of the most unsung, unpraised, unnoticed, and yet one of the most valuable assets in our society." Our dads hold the key to the unlocked door of our hearts. Love him for it!

"IN ANY FAMILY, LOVE IS THE OIL THAT EASES FRICTION, THE CEMENT THAT BINDS US CLOSE, AND THE MUSIC THAT BRINGS HARMONY."

-EVA BURROWS

9

WHY WE NEED EACH OTHER

Not all men have the privilege of parenting daughters, so those of us who have these little angels count ourselves blessed (most of the time). Sure our wallets are a bit lighter than men without daughters. We learn such minutiae as the difference between pillow shams and bed skirts. Yet, we also get the love, laughs, and smiles that can suddenly turn bad moments and stressful workdays into sheer joy!

As the oldest, Jenna and I have had the most time together. During her younger days, there were a couple years when she was the only child old enough to throw a football, swing a bat, or play soccer. The best part was that she *liked* me teaching her how to do those things! What more could I ask? Her early interest in sports was just the beginning of an athletic career that extended into high school softball. In between my travels, I did my best to be at her practices and games. I loved coaching her at home and practicing with her so she would continually improve. One year, her high school softball coach asked me to step in as the third-base coach. I had a blast! On the field, Jenna would listen to me when I told her to wait, run, or slide. Not because I was her boss who would tell her what to do, but because I was able to see what she couldn't. My life experience in the game of baseball had given me validity in her eyes and she trusted me to coach her.

Currently I'm enjoying immeasurable joy from my adult girls, more than I could have ever imagined. They are exactly what I need. Because they are in it, my life is richer and more rewarding. They are my biggest fans, supporters, and companions for my bride, Crystal, when I'm away. They are my best friends, with whom I can laugh and in whom I can confide.

Fathers, our daughters need us. The older they become the more they realize it. What's so great for me now is my perspective. For example, when our daughters are little girls they think we can "hang the moon." And before you know it…bang! The turbulent waters of the teen years! Hang in there when they arrive. Better days are coming.

Our family is praying that you apply the material and ideas in this book. Ask God for patience, wisdom and grace, and that your daughters will come full circle for you in the way mine have for me.

We have covered many topics in this book. We all have challenges and frustrations. We all have pressure points. We all get tired. And we all—fathers and daughters—need each other. Why? Because that's the way the heavenly Father designed us.

When no one else is there for her, you are. When she needs to go to dance class or cheerleading practice, you take her. When her heart gets broken, you comfort her. When she overdrafts her bank account, you teach her the wisest way to get back on her feet. When someone bullies her or makes her feel anything other than beautiful, cherished, and loved, you step in and protect her. That's what you were meant to do for her.

That is the privilege of being a father to girls. We are to fight. We are to stand. We are to be the protectors and the safe arms that hold her when the world tries to rip her apart. I love the way Gregory E. Lang says it when explaining why a daughter needs a dad: "Because a father is the man a girl loves first, and no girl ever forgets her first love."

ACTION STEPS

☑ Think positive! You may feel a baby step is not worth it, but it is. Want proof? Big doors swing on small hinges!

☑ Fathers, our daughters need us. They want us (the ones in their teens just don't realize it yet). No matter where you are at, engage in your daughter's life! Start by writing down two ideas for doing so.

1.

2.

☑ Prepare for battle. Fathering girls is no "walk in the park!" We are to be the protectors and the safe arms that hold her when the world tries to rip her apart. At the right time and in the proper tone of voice, share this with your daughter.

What My Dad Just Told Your Dad

by Grace Silva Rothrock

We all know we have a father somewhere. To what extent he chooses to be a parent to us is a different story. But across the board, regardless of age or lifestyle, I think it's safe to say that without a dad we all have a hole in our hearts. Dads and daughters do need each other, but I want to explore the truths behind why a daughter needs a good dad. If he plays an abusive, negative, or condescending role in her life, it can seem sometimes as if a girl is better off without her father.

One of the many reasons a good dad is so crucial is because we are all born with a desire to feel accepted, loved, and beautiful. Before it's time for a woman to be married and be with a man, her self-worth is often affirmed by her dad. The long-term effect of a positive, verbal, sweet father figure equals a more successful and confident woman. In most cases, girls have goals, dreams, and the confidence needed to accomplish them. A good father infuses self-esteem in his daughter.

Girls, dads play a huge part in our stability in life. When we have a present and active dad, it allows our femininity to blossom so we don't have gender-role confusion. It's a beautiful thing to be a lady. Good fathers cover that innate feeling of abandonment for girls, and they have the power to redeem and settle that fear in our hearts.

I understand that some of you happened to stumble across this book, or your parent is making you read this in hopes that it might spark a bond between you and your "#1 Man." But by now you might be thinking, "Grace, I want the kind of relationship with my dad like you talk about, but it's not that way for me. It's never going to work out that way for me."

I want you to know that I have faith in God and in you. Therefore, I believe differently for your life! I know that with prayer, hope, forgiveness, and patience, anything is possible. You are not alone. Change is around the corner. When we as women begin to treat our dads with respect and begin to be the kind of daughter we have always wanted to become, there is no greater feeling than to be at peace in relationships. Trust me, I've walked both sides of that street!

We need to be grateful for the fathers who value us, hold us in high esteem, and continually allow us to feel safe and secure in their presence. I think most of you ladies would agree with me that we don't want dads who are on the sidelines, but rather who are active and engaged in our lives. We want and need someone to be our hero—to fight for us, protect us, and be willing to give up his life for ours. When the time is right, share this with your dad.

Whether I was eleven or twenty-three, through the countless car breakdowns, heartbreaks, bank overdrafts, and other problems, I could always go to my dad. I didn't have to earn his love. He offered it freely and has always had the best intentions for my life.

I remember when I was buying my first car. It was a 1997 cherry-red, two-door Honda Civic with black interior, sunroof, and a spoiler. It was sporty, quick, and, of course, cute as can be. Dad helped me pick it out on the lot, negotiated good financing, and co-signed for the loan so I could establish credit. The next morning, I woke up excited to drive my new wheels, but when I turned the key in the ignition it wouldn't start. I ran inside and told Dad what had happened. He could see the disappointment and frustration all over my face. The car had a dead battery! So, my dad did what any hero would do. He put on his coat and took me back to the dealership. As he approached the salesman who sold us this "flawless vehicle," he shook his hand firmly, and said, "My daughter bought the red Honda here yesterday. To our surprise, there is a dead battery in it this morning. What can you do to help us? Because I'm not leaving until you make this situation right with my daughter."

Without someone to step in and defend me it would have been a much longer process and probably a different outcome. I needed my dad to step into my circumstance and make a world of difference—and he did!

ACTION STEPS

☑ Share with your dad why he is important to you.

☑ Embrace each other and live like you need each other, because you do!

☑ Pray for your dad every day. It may be surprising to you, but it's not easy for him to cultivate a thriving relationship with the Lord, flourish in his marriage with your mom, provide financially for his household, be successful at his work, maintain good health, and please his children all the time.

Believe me, you do not want your dad's responsibility. What you do want is to be his encourager, endorser, and daughter who provides joy and strength to help him carry his load so you don't have to!

EPILOGUE: NO GREATER LOVE

When Kristianna was five years old, she was initially diagnosed with a lemon-sized tumor growing in her throat. The mass was crushing her trachea and restricting 78 percent of her air supply. The preliminary biopsy report was not good. The diagnosis: rhabdomyosarcoma, a malignant tumor. I have never felt so desperate or helpless in my life. I remember looking at her fragile little body and crying out in desperation to God, "Take me instead! Take me instead!" If possible, I would have reached down her little throat, extracted the tumor, and swallowed it myself. I wanted to take her pain. I wanted to die in her place. I would have given my life in an instant so hers could be spared.

This, my friends, illustrates the love of a father's heart.

When I realized the emptiness that was staring me in the face, considering a life without my little girl seemed unbearable. I didn't think I would ever know joy again. In the very same way, God—our heavenly Father—loves us. Recognizing our wrongdoing and the terminal tumor called sin, our heavenly Father created a plan. He sent His Son, Jesus Christ, to reach down our spiritual throats and extract the malignant tumor, thus saving our lives. Why? Because of love. This is a father's love for His own!

Jesus died on the cross for the sins of the world. Jesus did what I couldn't do for Kristianna. He took the tumor of sin and extracted it, bearing it on the cross. He died in our place to spare our lives. My friend, if you know about Jesus Christ but are not positive you know Him personally, then I beg you to stop and pray this prayer with me now: "Lord Jesus, God's Son, I know that I am a sinner. I know that only You have the ability to save me from my sin by dying in my place on the cross. Right now, I place my faith and trust in You alone for my eternal salvation. Thank You for reaching down into my 'throat,' eliminating my terminal tumor of sin to give me life by faith alone in Jesus Christ. Amen."

I guarantee that little prayer will be the most transformational moment of your life. Write to me (msteam@mikesilva.org). Let me know of your prayer of commitment, and I'll send you a gift that will inspire, help, and encourage you.

Men, if you love your daughter with an unending, sacrificial love, then there's nothing you cannot accomplish! Leave room for error. Forgive and forget. Do not hold grudges and accept her for who she is, and watch her reciprocate. Be the #1 man you desire to be because she needs you. Anyone can be a father, but no one else can be her daddy.

May your father-daughter relationship be centered around a perfect love that is made possible only through Jesus Christ. He first loved us, so now we can have the capacity to love each other. Remember, the Bible says, "Love covers over a multitude of sin" (1 Pet. 4:8). Praise God that we are saved because God's Son swallowed the malignant tumor for us!

—Mike Silva

1 John 4:7-19 (NASB)

Beloved, let us love one another, for love is from God; and everyone who loves is born of God and knows God.

The one who does not love does not know God, for God is love.

By this the love of God was manifested in us, that God has sent His only begotten Son into the world so that we might live through Him.

In this is love, not that we loved God, but that He loved us and sent His Son to be the propitiation for our sins.

Beloved, if God so loved us, we also ought to love one another.

No one has seen God at any time; if we love one another, God abides in us, and His love is perfected in us.

By this we know that we abide in Him and He in us, because He has given us of His Spirit.

We have seen and testify that the Father has sent the Son to be the Savior of the world.

Whoever confesses that Jesus is the Son of God, God abides in him, and he in God.

We have come to know and have believed the love which God has for us. God is love, and the one who abides in love abides in God, and God abides in him.

By this, love is perfected with us, so that we may have confidence in the day of judgment; because as He is, so also are we in this world.

There is no fear in love; but perfect love casts out fear, because fear involves punishment, and the one who fears is not perfected in love.

We love, because He first loved us.

Resources

1. "Strengthening Father Daughter Relationships" by Wayne Parker, from about.com guide, 7 April 2010. Found at http://fatherhood.about.com/od/daughersanddads/a/daughters.htm.

2. "Top Ten Ways to Stay Close to Your Daughter as She Grows Up" by Wayne Parker, from about.com guide, 2 April 2010. Found at http://fatherhood.about.com/od/daughersanddads/a/closetodaughter.htm.

3. *The Five Love Languages: The Secret to Love That Lasts* by Gary Chapman. Chicago: Northfield Publishing, 1994, 1995, 2004, 2010.

4. Written interview with "Sam," 21 December 2009.

5. Phone interview with "Mary," 5 May 2010.

6. "Understanding Stepfamilies" by J. Larson, the National Stepfamily Resource Center. From *American Demographics* 14, 360, 1992.

7. "Is There Hope for the American Marriage?"by Caitlin Flanagan, *Time* magazine, 2 July 2009. Found at http://www.time.com/time/nation/article/0,8599,1908243,00.html.

8. *The Purpose Driven Life: What on Earth Am I Here For?* by Rick Warren. Grand Rapids, Mich.: Zondervan, 2002, 72.

GET TO KNOW MORE ABOUT MIKE SILVA—
VISIT WWW.MIKESILVA.ORG TODAY!

www.mikesilva.org (English)

www.mikesilvafestival.com (Español)

http://twitter.com/MikeSilvaLive

http://facebook.com/MikeSilvaTeam

BE A #1 MAN

JOIN THE CONVERSATION AT

WWW.FACEBOOK.COM/NUMBERONEMAN

LISTEN TO A PERSONAL AUDIO CD, *DADDY'S LITTLE GIRL*, FEATURING MIKE AT A FATHER-DAUGHTER CONFERENCE AT HUME LAKE CHRISTIAN CAMPS IN CALIFORNIA.

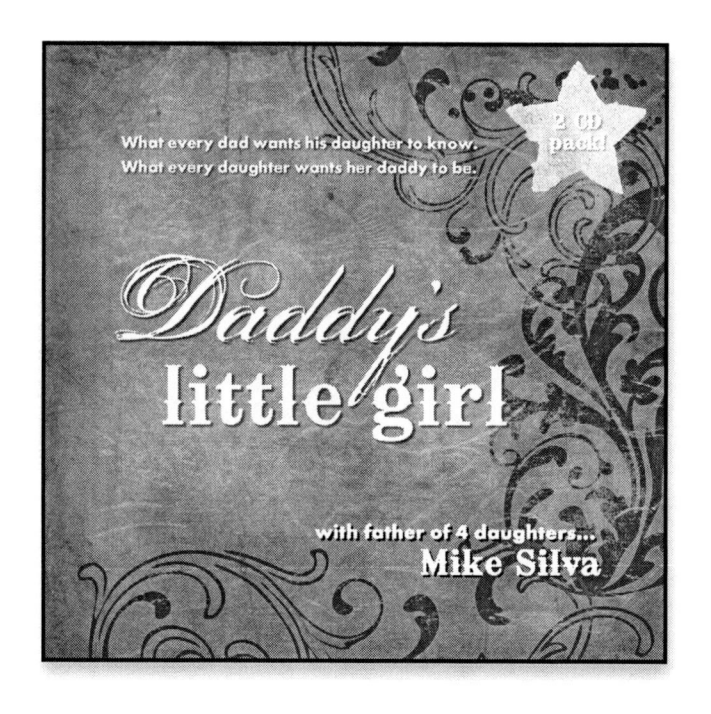

Order yours at:

www.mikesilva.org/resources/books